Always Looking Up

ALSO BY MICHAEL J. FOX

Lucky Man

MICHAEL J. FOX

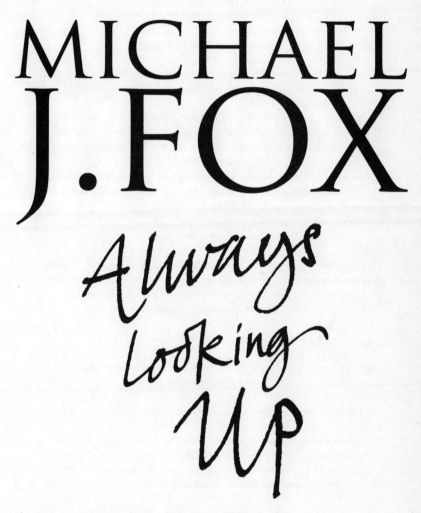

Always Looking Up

The Adventures of an Incurable Optimist

EBURY
PRESS

1 3 5 7 9 10 8 6 4 2

Published in 2009 by Ebury Press, an imprint of Ebury Publishing
A Random House Group company
First published in the USA by Hyperion in 2009

Copyright © Michael J. Fox 2009

Michael J. Fox has asserted his right to be identified as the author of this Work
in accordance with the Copyright, Designs and Patents Act 1988

'Sheila.' Copyright 1962 Sony/ATV Music Publishing LLC. All rights
administered by Sony/ATV Music Publishing LLC, 8 Music Square West,
Nashville, TN 37203. All rights reserved. Used by permission.

'Glory Days' by Bruce Springsteen. Copyright © 1984 Bruce Springsteen
(ASCAP). Reprinted by permission. International copyright secured.
All rights reserved.

'Magic Bus' lyrics by permission of Pete Townshend.

All rights reserved. No part of this publication may be reproduced, stored in
a retrieval system, or transmitted in any form or by any means, electronic,
mechanical, photocopying, recording or otherwise, without the
prior permission of the copyright owner

The Random House Group Limited Reg. No. 954009

Addresses for companies within the Random House Group can be found at
www.randomhouse.co.uk

A CIP catalogue record for this book is available from the British Library

The Random House Group Limited supports The Forest Stewardship Council
(FSC), the leading international forest certification organisation. All our titles
that are printed on Greenpeace approved FSC certified paper carry the FSC logo.
Our paper procurement policy can be found at www.rbooks.co.uk/environment

Printed in Australia by Griffin Press

ISBN 9780091928261

To buy books by your favourite authors and register for offers visit
www.rbooks.co.uk

For Tracy, Sam, Aquinnah, Schuyler, and Esmé.

And for Karen.

With love.

Contents

Prologue

© John Huba/Art + Commerce

In the opening pages of *Lucky Man*, I described a morning in Florida nineteen years ago when I woke up with a hangover and a twitching left pinky finger. In the intervening years, my life has seen many changes. Most mornings, for example, I awake to find my left pinky finger perfectly still—it's the rest of my body that's shaking uncontrollably. Technically, my body is only fully at peace when my mind is completely at rest—that is, asleep. Low brain activity means fewer neurons firing, or in my case, misfiring. As I awaken, before my conscious mind really knows what's happening, my body has already gotten the news in the form of insistent neural instructions to twist, twitch, and contort. Any chance of slipping back into sleep is lost.

This morning Tracy is already up, dealing out breakfasts and readying the kids for school. I blindly fumble a plastic vial from the nightstand, dry-swallow a couple of pills, and then fall immediately into the first series of actions that, while largely automatic, demand a practiced determination. I swing my legs around to the side of the bed, and the instant my feet hit the floor, the two of them are in an argument. A condition called "dystonia," a regular complement to Parkinson's, cramps my feet severely and curls them inward, pressing my ankles toward the floor and the soles of my feet toward each other as though they were about to close together in prayer. I snake my right foot out toward the edge of the rug and toe-hook one of my hard leather loafers. I force my foot into the shoe, repeat the process with the left, and then cautiously stand up. Chastened by the unyielding confines of the leather, my feet begin to behave themselves. The spasms have stopped, but the aching will persist for the next twenty minutes or so.

First stop: the bathroom. I'll spare you the initial details of my visit, except to say that with PD, it is essential to put the seat up. Grasping the toothpaste is nothing compared to the effort it takes to coordinate the two-handed task of wrangling the toothbrush and strangling out a line of paste onto the bristles. By now, my right hand has started up again, rotating at the wrist in a circular motion, perfect for what I'm about to do. My left hand guides my right hand up to my mouth, and once the back of the Oral-B touches the inside of my upper lip, I let go. It's like releasing the tension on a slingshot and compares favorably to the most powerful state-of-the-art electric toothbrush on the market. With no off switch, stopping means seizing my right wrist with my left hand, forcing it down to the sink basin, and shaking the brush loose as though disarming a knife-wielding attacker. I can usually tell whether shaving is a good idea on any particular day, and this morning, like most, I decide it's too early to risk bloodshed. I opt for a quick pass with an electric stubble trimmer. *Miami Vice* lives.

A bench in the shower takes the pressure off my feet, and the steady drumbeat of the water on my back has a therapeutic effect, though if I sit here much longer, I might never get up. Getting dressed is made easier by the pills, which have begun to assert their influence. I avoid clothing with too many buttons or laces, although I'm still addicted to Levi's 501s, making me a fashion victim in the truest sense of the word. In lieu of proper brushing, I raise my twitching fingers up to my hairline and, raking it back, hope for the best. Executing a slow shuffle (my legs haven't yet earned my trust for the day), I make my way out to greet my family.

At the turn from our bedroom into the hallway, there is an old full-length mirror in a wooden frame. I can't help but catch a glimpse of myself as I pass. Turning fully toward the glass, I consider what I see. This reflected version of myself, wet, shaking, rumpled, pinched, and slightly stooped, would be alarming were it not for the self-satisfied expression pasted across my face. I would ask the obvious question, "What are you smiling about?," but I already know the answer: "It just gets better from here."

. . .

How to Lose Your Brain Without Losing Your Mind—that was my original title for the memoir written eight years ago. On the second or third page of the earliest draft, I made reference to myself as being a "lucky man." After a few edits, I kept going back to those two words, and eventually they found their way onto the cover of the book. They fit then, and they still do now.

As the title for this new book, *Always Looking Up* works on a couple of levels. First off—let's just get this one out of the way—it's a short joke. At a fraction of an inch under five-foot-five, much of my interaction with the world and the people in it has required that I tilt my head backward and direct my gaze upward. However, this isn't a manifesto about the hardships of the vertically challenged. Frankly, my height or lack thereof never bothered me much. Although there's no doubt that it's contributed to a certain mental toughness. I've made the most of the head start one gains from being underestimated. And that's more to the point of it—*Always Looking Up* alludes to an emotional, psychological, intellectual, and spiritual outlook that has served me throughout my life and, perhaps, even saved me throughout my life with Parkinson's. It's not that I don't feel the aching pain of loss. Physical strength, spontaneity, physical balance, manual dexterity, the freedom to do the work I want to do when I want to do it, the confidence that I can always be there for my family when they need me—all of these have been, if not completely lost to Parkinson's, at least drastically compromised.

The last ten years of my life, which is really the stuff of this book, began with such a loss: my retirement from *Spin City*. I found myself struggling with a strange new dynamic: the shifting of public and private personas. I had been Mike the actor, then Mike the actor with PD. Now was I just Mike with PD? Parkinson's had consumed my career and, in a sense, had become my career. But where did all of this leave *me*? I had to build a new life when I was already pretty happy with the old one. I'd been blessed with a twenty-five-year career in a job that I loved. I had a brilliant, beautiful, funny, supportive wife and an expanding brood of irrepressible kids. If I had to give up any part of this, how could I possibly protect myself from losing all of it?

The answer had very little to do with "protection" and everything to do with perspective. The only unavailable choice was whether or not to have Parkinson's. Everything else was up to me. I could concentrate on the loss—rush in with whatever stopgap measures my ego could manufacture. I could rely on my old friend from the nineties, denial. Or I could just get on with my life and see if maybe those holes started filling in themselves. Over the last ten years, they have, in the most amazing ways.

What follows is a memoir of this last decade. But unlike *Lucky Man*, it is thematic rather than chronological. Starting Over (*work*), Speaking Out (*politics*), Seeking Answers (*faith*), Safe at Home (*family*). These are the struts of my existence. These are the critical supports of my life.

Together they form a bulwark against the ravages of Parkinson's disease. My identity has so much to do with my ability to self-express, to assert my creativity and productive worth, my rights and the rights of whatever communities I'm a part of and therefore responsible to, my freedom to seek spiritual purpose and to explore the complex bonds I share with those I love most and without whom I would have long since succumbed to darker forces.

While not a strict narrative, *Always Looking Up* describes a journey of self-discovery and reinvention. The story is a testament to the consolations that get me through and give meaning to every area of my life.

For everything this disease has taken, something with greater value has been given—sometimes just a marker that points me in a new direction that I might not otherwise have traveled. So, sure, it may be one step forward and two steps back, but after a time with Parkinson's, I've learned that what is important is making that one step count; always looking up.

PART ONE

Starting Over

ALANFIL

Into the Great Wide Open

In many ways, day-to-day life is tougher now than it was when *Lucky Man* was published. I thought I was in rough shape in 2000 when I retired from *Spin City*. The twin hammers of producing and performing in one hundred episodes over a four-year span had knocked me on my ass. Brain surgery two years earlier had reduced the emphatic tremor on my left side but had done nothing to diminish the trembling on my right and in my legs. Titrating medication was a daily battle with a shape-shifting enemy. The segues between being "on" and "off" my meds, transitions that under ideal circumstances transpired like quasi-civil conversations, had deteriorated into a belligerent riot of interruptions and cross talk. In a futile attempt to be "on" at the optimal times—that is, when I was performing—I would try to get through my producing duties with as little levodopa (or "L-Dopa," the synthetic dopamine that Parkinson's patients take to control symptoms) in my system as possible, so that when I had to act, I could up the dose and be steady in front of the cameras. Rarely, if ever, did I get it right. Getting it wrong—erring on the side of too much levodopa—brought on a torrent of dyskinesias; uncontrollable movements like undulating, weaving, rocking, and bobbing. The cruel joke was that I didn't notice it as much going through my paces as I did afterward when I watched the footage in the editing room.

Having decided halfway through the fourth season that my physical condition would not allow me to do a fifth, I began to wonder if I'd even make it through the thirteen or so episodes that remained. My daily regimen of drugs (which, by the way, have no psychotropic effect—no buzz whatsoever) affected my speech patterns and sometimes caused me to slur my words or hesitate before saying my lines—a real bitch when you're trying to time a joke. As for physical comedy, hell, I was just trying to avoid physical tragedy.

Although everyone—cast, crew, and audience—knew by this point that I had Parkinson's, I was still attempting to play a character who did not. Whatever comedic or dramatic complexity a particular scene called for, my greatest acting challenge was always acting like I didn't have Parkinson's. Though I continued to employ the same old bag of tricks that had served me for years—manipulating hand props to control tremulous hands, leaning against walls, desks, and fellow actors, shifting in a chair or behind a table to cover my uncontrollable leg and foot movements—the advance in symptoms was forcing me to update my repertoire. I discovered that, for short periods of time, I could direct all the energy coursing through my body to one particular extremity—a hand, leg, or foot. So when blocking a scene, I would position myself (and the rest of the cast as well) in such a way as to best conceal the appendage in which the surge of Parkinsonian energy was manifest. Like I said, it's the same sort of thing I'd been doing for years, and my thinking was that once I could explain to people why I was doing it, it would make the whole process that much smoother.

But it didn't make it any easier. It was still tough. Now people just had a better idea of why it was tough. My friend Michael Boatman played Carter Heywood, the mayor's minority affairs liaison on the show. One day we were rehearsing a scene that required both of us to pass through the mayor's office door simultaneously and in opposite directions. Scripts in hand, we started to walk the scene, but when we both got to the door, instead of passing by Michael, I froze directly in front of him. "You gotta move," I said, rather more bluntly than intended.

Michael is one of the nicest guys on the planet, but he was a little confused and taken aback by my direction. "What?" he replied.

"You gotta move. I can't move until you move."

He eventually complied, and after the rehearsal, I tried to explain what had just happened.

Occasionally, when my brain asks my body to perform simple tasks that involve some degree of judgment regarding spatial relationships, the message gets lost in transmission. It takes some form of outside stimulus, like the movement of an obstacle or, curiously, even the introduction of an obstacle, for me to move forward. Some Parkies who freeze when walking can resume again when a ruler is placed in front of their feet and they are forced to step over it. Michael, of course, accepted my explanation and even managed to laugh with me about the strangeness of it all.

Over the course of a day, a week, a month, a year, countless situations would arise when similar explanations were required, and that, in and of itself, became a fatiguing responsibility. The Jekyll-and-Hyde difference between when the meds were working and when they weren't understandably confused people. Those around me had a difficult time reconciling the energetic, expressive Mike Flaherty that they would see in front of the camera with the shuffling, masked-face Mike Fox that they would encounter as he went about his business behind the scenes. My producing partner, Nelle Fortenberry, remembers more than a few occasions when department heads and other members of the cast and crew would step into her office, close the door, and beg her to tell them why I was mad at them.

"What makes you think he's mad at you?" she would reply.

"I just passed him in the hallway, and he didn't smile or wave or even slow down."

Nelle would repeatedly explain that one of the symptoms of PD is a dearth of facial animation—the Parkinson's mask. In addition, something as simple as turning my head over my shoulder to convey a greeting can be an actual physical impossibility. Once I have any degree of momentum while walking, the expenditure of energy required to stop and start again can be ten times as taxing as it is for a normal-brained person.

Away from the set, it was Nelle with whom I most often interacted on a day-to-day basis, along with executive producers Bill Lawrence and David Rosenthal, and our director, Andy Cadiff. This was when I put on my producing hat, and we'd wade through production budgets, future story lines, script drafts, proposals for set designs, post-production issues, cast and crew grievances, and the rest of the minutiae that comes with churning out a new episode of television every seven days. Believe it or not, it could be fun. But it could also be grueling. Problems were like popcorn; as we worked our way through the bowl we had in front of us, it seemed like there was a big popper outside the office door, constantly manufacturing a new batch.

Sometimes I'd laugh when Nelle would lay out the new challenges for the day. I'd remind her that, however big the problems were, they wouldn't be *my* biggest. I didn't mean this as a complaint but as a comment on a perspective I'd gained from my situation.

If I could go back today and speak to the me of 2000, as I waged my daily battles with Parkinson's disease, I'd have this to say: "You ain't seen nothing yet!"

In fact, having the benefit of my experience since, I know now that it was going to get a lot worse before it got . . . well . . . a lot worse. Still, with what I have learned since about managing stress through creative scheduling, and the current generation of drugs that were just around the corner, I probably could have done a full seven seasons. That's not to say for a minute that I wish I had. My decision to leave *Spin City* was the right call at the right time.

By then, making a decision about what to commit my time and energy to came down to how I felt about something as opposed to what I thought about it. Certainly, my decision to retire from *Spin City* in the spring of 2000, effective at the end of the fourth season, was all "feel."

The decision happened late in the afternoon on the last day of the twentieth century. My family and I were snorkeling the pristine waters off St. John's in the U.S. Virgin Islands. We'd been visiting this beach for years, and had never seen a sea turtle. Having finally spotted one gliding through the sea grass just inside the coral reef, I swam slowly behind it, keeping a respectful distance. When I finally emerged from the water, I kicked off my flippers, walked over to where Tracy was toweling off the kids, grabbed a towel for myself, and informed her that I was leaving the show. It may have been a bone-deep exhaustion from battling symptoms every day just to do my job, or maybe it was just the sublime indifference of that turtle, but a switch had flipped, and depending on how I chose to accept it, a light had either just turned on or just turned off. If the perfunctory nature of my announcement startled Tracy, she covered it well. Certainly it was her moment to fill. She could have laughed it off like a weak throwaway joke or just pretended to ignore it, tacitly offering me the space to reconsider. Or she could have said, "Are you out of your fucking mind?" After all, what I was so casually proposing would bring about sweeping changes in each of our lives, as well as the kids'. I didn't even mention the turtle, fearing that she would think I was only consulting her for a second opinion. Whatever rough patches there had been in our marriage had usually arisen when one of us—okay, me—acted unilaterally. Bottom line, she could have reacted in any of a number of ways. But what she did was look me in the eye, utter a single word, "Good," and pull me into a wet, sandy embrace.

For the few remaining days of the vacation, we didn't talk about it much. If I was waiting for her to talk me out of it, that wasn't happening.

But could the break really have been that simple, that clean? This was a momentous decision, easily one of the most important in my life, and I was just blurting it out.

Well, yes—in a sense. Never once after my encounter with the sea turtle have I wavered in my conviction that it was the right thing for me to do and the right time for me to do it. But it was hard too. Not a hard decision to make, but a hard decision to have made. As with any turning point or instance when a new road is chosen and an old one forsaken, there are consequences. Here it was, New Year's Eve, the cusp of not only a new year, but a new millennium, and my resolution was to leave behind everything that I had resolved to achieve, acquire, and accumulate over the previous twenty years. I knew I wouldn't just be leaving the show—I would be putting aside my life as an actor. While I always had difficulty thinking of myself as an artist, I took pride in being a craftsman. I think I understood that even though, officially, my retirement was from *Spin City* and not my career as a whole, I couldn't just tweak the schedule or the working conditions and expect to take on another leading role in a television series or film. This was it. I was essentially pulling the plug. Adios. Bye-bye.

John Gielgud, revered for his decades on the English stage and famous for playing Dudley Moore's butler in *Arthur,* once described his life's work in this way: "Acting is half shame, half glory. Shame at exhibiting yourself, glory when you can forget yourself." As a sixteen-year-old, just embarking upon a career, I could relate. I dabbled in the other arts, for a time envisioning a future as a writer, commercial artist, or musician, but it was acting that came most naturally to me. At an age when most people (and I was no exception) feel ungainly, awkward, and unlovable, I'd found something for which I seemed to have a facility. I could be anyone, anything, any size, any shape, transport myself to any place or time. And if I did it right, there was the bonus of approbation from those whom I was otherwise hard-pressed to please. Roles in school plays and locally produced film and television productions encouraged me to test my potential, and soon I became more and more aware that my real limitations were geographical. I needed to go to where the work was.

Acting provided a life beyond anything I could imagine— and I had a fervent imagination. At eighteen, my aspirations led me to Los Angeles. I stuck through humiliating and seemingly pointless auditions and routine rejections, with the occasional reward of a small TV gig or national commercial that would pay my rent and keep my spirits afloat. Then came success, and with it a new confidence in my craftsmanship and the courage to try new things; some with positive results, some not so positive, but never with regret.

Acting was an occupation that required me to be both an observer and participant in the world. Throughout my many years in comedy, I relied upon an intuitive ability to find the humor in almost any situation. There's always a "funny part." An actor's palette is the entirety of the human experience. A career as long and busy as mine had allowed me to empathize and connect with people in a way no other profession could have. And of course, there were the tangible benefits: travel, a financial windfall, goodwill beyond any deserving. Perhaps the greatest gift of all came courtesy of a fortuitous piece of casting: meeting Tracy on the set of *Family Ties*.

I never went to college; I didn't even finish high school. Being an actor was the only career I'd known, and now, on the inferred advice of a turtle, I was ready to leave it as easily as I had toweled the seawater off my sunburned back?

Deep down I knew that my love of working—that mega-volt crackle that licked up my spine when a well-written joke was well-timed and well-received—was still there. A hard-earned comfort had developed after so many years of performing—not laziness, but a reasonable confidence that no matter what emotion, intention, or attitude I needed to access, that arrow would be in my quiver when I reached for it. As a younger actor, I could sometimes obscure my insecurity about the integrity of a given moment with some deft piece of physicality: Alex Keaton, putting his hands in his pockets and leaping backward onto the kitchen counter; Marty McFly, duck-walking, windmilling, and power-sliding through "Johnny B. Goode"; Brantley Foster, hulk-flexing in the elevator clad only in boxer shorts; or even Mike Flaherty, stripping off his sweat-pants in midair while executing a full flip over the bed and his waiting girlfriend. I could always rely on the physical. The unfortunate irony was that at a time when I felt in full pos-session of the emotional and intellectual dimensions of my performing identity, I could no longer count on my body to play along. I didn't want to make choices as an actor based on disability rather than ability.

Although I can't claim any lucid memories of the evening, I'm pretty sure I spent New Year's Eve of 1979, my first as a young actor living in California, getting drunk off my ass and making wild resolutions about all that I would accomplish in the coming decades. Now, twenty years later, enjoying a quiet, sober tropical New Year's Eve with my family and reflecting upon all that young man had accomplished, I prepared to step into an uncertain future.

SOUNDSTAGE D, CHELSEA PIERS

MARCH 17, 2000

For a television series, especially a sitcom, one hundred episodes represents an important threshold. Traditionally, the century mark is the minimum required to successfully launch a show into syndication. Going into season four, we expected, according to our twenty-two-show schedule, to finish the season with ninety-six shows in the can.

Our syndication deal was already in place, so it wasn't technically crucial that we produce those extra four. But while at peace with my decision to leave the show, I became fixated on that milestone. This could have meant adding another month of production for which we had neither the time nor the money. So, rather than allowing myself to ease out of the show, I had created a logistical conundrum that required sometimes shooting one and a half shows per week, thus being able to bank six episodes in four weeks. The plan was for a one-hour finale, edited into two shows for syndication. Filmed over two weeks, for the most part without a studio audience, the storyline would also call for a day of location shooting in Washington, DC. All of this pre-filmed material, rough-edited and assembled, could then be screened for the final New York studio audience with live scenes interspersed.

I'm sure it was a difficult period for the cast and the crew, although for the last month and a half of the season, we knew that my leaving would mark not the end of *Spin City* but, rather, a transition. The show would continue. Charlie Sheen signed on as the new deputy mayor, and production would be moved to Los Angeles, where Charlie and *Spin City* co-creator Gary Goldberg lived. (Gary would reassume executive producer duties.) Of course, this would be the New York–based crew's final season. For the audience, then, this would not be a farewell to the show, just a farewell to the character of Mike Flaherty.

The final episode was tricky to conceive and execute because the entire situation was rife with verisimilitude. Mike Flaherty, for reasons that were not entirely fair, was being forced to prematurely leave the job he loved. I could relate, and the other actors seemed as concerned for me as their alter egos were for Mike. It was all one and the same. This was it. It was really over.

The fictional Mike Flaherty's prospects were better than mine. He'd probably work again. But would I? Doubtful. At least, not like this, performing week-in, week-out, in front of a live studio audience.

I worked closely with David Rosenthal, Bill Lawrence, and the rest of the writing staff to ensure that Mike would have at least one substantial scene with each of the show's regular characters. This was both to give the audience a sense of closure on each of these relationships and to allow me one last chance to share the stage with each of these gifted performers, whom I had come to care so much about over the previous four years. The whole thing was loaded with emotion; the logistical burden we'd created only compounded the exhaustion that had me retiring in the first place. Beyond the soundstage, my plans to leave the show created another wave of support and affection comparable to what I'd experienced two years earlier when I made public my PD diagnosis. There was a tremendous media interest in those last days of my tenure, with members of the press on set, observing our prep for my final show. Everyone—cast, crew, writers, and production staff—was at once at the top of his or her game and in a total fog. But they, at least, grasped something that seemed to be eluding me. This final episode marked a turning point in my life, a tectonic shift. I might have looked around, understood what had been set in motion and what would soon grind to a halt, and said, "Oh, shit! What have I done?"

I had sailed into waters too narrow and too shallow to turn the boat around. It's not that I was totally unaware of what was happening; I was caught up in the emotion like everyone else. And I felt guilty too, knowing that by choosing to change my life's direction, I had thrown so many others off course; hopefully not irreversibly, but probably unexpectedly. Or maybe it wasn't so unexpected. Everyone could see my battle fatigue. And the final push to bring it all to a close in a fitting way, the pressure to hit the one-hundred-episode mark, and the physical demands of simultaneously performing and producing only reinforced the ultimate wisdom of my decision. But the imperative that I get these last few laughs and collapse across the finish line precluded any thoughts about what I was falling into on the other side of that invisible threshold. For now, what drove me to keep going was the need to stop.

Even if I didn't appear to be saying, "Oh, shit!," I did it by proxy. In order to find a way for Mike Flaherty to leave his job at City Hall (and for me to leave *Spin City*), we had to create that moment for him, and this safe remove provided me with a little perspective.

This was the conceit: Though innocent of any wrongdoing himself, the mayor of New York is implicated in a scandal linking City Hall to organized crime. Seeing no way to spin his boss out of the jam, Mike's only recourse is to take the fall himself. He agrees to resign from his post. His coworkers are shocked, and he himself is shaken, but he is also certain that leaving is the only right thing to do. And so he goes about severing his ties to the job that has defined him. After his last day at work, at home with his girlfriend and coworker Caitlin, Mike voices his anxiety. What the hell is he going to do now?

```
CAITLIN IS PLACING FOOD ON THE TABLE — DINNER FOR
TWO. MICHAEL ENTERS.


                    Caitlin
Hi.



                    Michael
Hey, you didn't make it to the bar.



                    Caitlin
Things were a little crazy at the office.



                    Michael
Yeah, I heard they lost somebody pretty valu-
able today.
```

Caitlin

He was just eye candy.

I've often felt that Heather Locklear is underestimated as an actress, for the most part because she's so natural and effortless in front of the camera. Further proof of her ability, though, was right in front of me as we worked on this last episode. Caitlin might have been a rock, but Heather was a mess, crying before and after every take. She was great that week, as she had been throughout the season. Brought in, after all, to help lighten my load as the going got tougher, Heather had done a spectacular job, just as Caitlin was doing for the soon-to-be-former deputy mayor.

The exchange that closed the scene, however, was really all about me and Tracy, an acknowledgment of how much I am empowered by her belief in me, in the life and family we have built together. Sometimes I have only the courage of her convictions, her unflinching support, and her assurance, almost matter-of-fact, that I should trust my heart, my gut, and her love. Reprising not just a moment from our recent history together, the words and emotions evoked remembrances of other times when I had offered my doubts and fears to my wife—drinking, career crises, Parkinson's—and she had not judged them, just shared them. When all appears lost, I look to Tracy to help me find it again—or, better yet, be with me for as long as it takes for something new to arrive. And longer.

MICHAEL SITS DOWN AT THE TABLE. FOR THE FIRST TIME IN A LONG WHILE HE TAKES A DEEP BREATH.

Michael

You know what, it's okay. I'm gonna bounce back from this, right?

Caitlin

Of course, Mike.

Michael

It's not over, right?

Caitlin

It's a long way from over.

Michael

It's weird, for as long as I can remember, every morning I've had somewhere to go, something to do. What am I going to do tomorrow when that alarm goes off?

Caitlin

I wouldn't set it.

On show night, the place was packed. The press was there and so was everyone from the network and the studio; my family had flown in from Vancouver; and all of the writers and producers who had worked on the show over the last four years had returned to say good-bye. Even with all the special guests, seats had been saved for regular civilians, those loyal audience members who had shown up every show night since the beginning. And of course, Tracy spent most of the evening just offstage, by the floor monitors with Gary, both of them in tears as they watched the episode and this chapter of our lives come to a close.

At the end of the night, I ran out to join the cast for curtain call, which we planned to include as part of the episode. I wore Mike Flaherty's Fordham letterman's jacket and embraced each of the cast members and waved good-bye. Behind all of this played the song "Glory Days," which Bruce Springsteen had kindly given us permission to use. It was a sentimental choice, but it was also meant to be ironic. *Time slips away and leaves you with nothing, mister, but boring stories of Glory Days.* Surely, my glory days hadn't come to an end. I would have more stories to tell.

After the show, we packed into a nearby restaurant we had booked for that night. We danced and partied, laughed our asses off, and said our good-byes. That night when Tracy and I got home and went to bed, I didn't set the alarm.

Shaking but Stirred

When I was diagnosed in 1991, I was determined to absorb the blow, suck up all the fear, pain, confusion, and doubt, and be grateful that a small group of friends and family were there to catch whatever spilled over. I understood that symptoms were a lagging indicator of the disease's progress, and that gave me the time and privacy I needed to process the situation. Similarly, when I disclosed my condition in 1998, after seven years of measuring the size and weight of the burden I had been carrying, I was, for the most part, just seeking relief from the strain. While nervous about how people were going to react when I told them the truth, I was far more concerned with their reactions if I continued to withhold it.

To be brutally honest, for much of that time, I was the only person in the world with Parkinson's. Of course, I mean that in the abstract. I had become acutely aware of people around me who appeared to have the symptoms of Parkinson's disease, but as long as they didn't know to identify with me, I was in no rush to identify with them. My situation allowed, if not complete denial, at least a thick padding of insulation. That would change.

I didn't burst out of this isolation with an agenda. Going public was a difficult decision, and I had misgivings. My subjective experience was now an objective fact in the wider world. It didn't belong to just me anymore—though I quickly learned that it hadn't belonged to just me in the first place. More than a million other Americans and their families were going through the same thing; some openly, some in secret due to concerns of being misunderstood and marginalized. I represented something to them, and whether any of us would have planned it this way, I now represented them in the minds of other people.

I recognized both a responsibility to this new community as well as an opportunity to do something positive. I could relate to the patients who wrote to me, particularly those online in Parkinson's chat rooms. (I did this mostly under an invented *nom de PD,* but it would get awkward when they'd ask me what

I thought of *me*.) One of the biggest revelations was, in spite of all our common travails, how different our experiences could be. Parkinson's disease takes many forms—for some reason, everyone gets their own version. A drug therapy or surgery that works for one may not work for another. Our reactions—emotional, psychological, and physical—vary greatly, and this obviously affects our ability to cope.

My interactions with the larger PD population put another dimension of my good fortune into stark relief. For whatever reason, I had been spared the torture of depression. By this, I don't mean that I hadn't had bouts of sadness, fear, or anxiety about my situation, although at times I had to cut through a layer of denial to recognize it. But clinical depression is a common symptom faced by approximately 40 percent of PD patients. Like dementia, it may be present from the beginning, appear over time, or show up suddenly in the later stages. As I said though, apart from the expected ups and downs of a life with Parkinson's, I don't struggle with the chemical imbalance that triggers severe depression.

I never logged out of the online PD forums without realizing how fortunate I was. My family, my relative youth, my financial situation, as well as my public position gave me a tremendous advantage in dealing with my illness. While Parkinson's did have a direct impact on my ability to do my job, I was, for all intents and purposes, my own boss. So for me, decisions like whether or not to disclose my illness were not as fraught with risk. The anonymity of the Internet also allowed me to see the impact my disclosure had on other patients, their families, and the people they interacted with on a daily basis. I'm sure that the effect would have been the same had it been any number of other well-known people, but just that someone with the ability to attract so much public interest had shone a light on their predicament meant more than I could have foreseen. *Okay,* I thought, *so what do I do with that?*

Within a few months of my disclosure, I began integrating myself into the Parkinson's patient community and familiarizing myself with the various organizations and foundations that had reached out to me. I invited a few representatives over to my apartment to discuss their programs and lay out how I might fit into their plans. While they were certainly professional, dedicated, and committed, I was still looking for a more aggressive focus on research moving forward toward a cure. One contingent, a group from the Parkinson's Action Network (PAN) led by Joan Samuelson, a young-onset PD patient and activist attorney, touched on those issues right away, as well as the disparity between federal funding for Parkinson's research as compared with other diseases.

The Senate Appropriations Subcommittee on Labor, Health, and Human Services had scheduled a hearing in Washington a few weeks later, and Joan presented a case that my testimony could bring attention to the issue and possibly move the dial on the support from Congress. Seeing a chance to make a difference, I agreed to testify.

What is now public record was little known at the time: I am a political junkie. As a preteen, I was inspired by Canadian Prime Minister Pierre Trudeau and frightened by President Richard Nixon. As a teenager, I volunteered for the British Columbia Liberal Party in the provincial elections, distributing my candidate's yard signs and redistributing his opponent's into the dumpster behind the liquor store. (It didn't help—my guy got thumped on election night.)

Throughout all those years, I followed politics avidly, and tried to stay informed about politicians and public policy. However, because I left Canada on my eighteenth birthday and was never a full-time resident again, and because I didn't become an American citizen until 2000, I had never cast a vote in any election. And without a vote of my own, I didn't feel I had the right to influence anyone else's.

By the time of the Congressional hearing, however, I was well on my way to becoming an American citizen. My papers were being processed, so I had no problem speaking my piece. By no means an expert on the current state of scientific research, I would speak to the effect this disease has on Americans, would share our hopes and hardships, assert our rights, and outline our expectations. Writing my congressional testimony was probably my first concentrated effort to communicate what I'd lived with for the last eight years. I didn't want people to walk away from my testimony muttering, "Poor bastard." Rather, I hoped they would be thinking, "Maybe we can do this."

The optimism that I carried into the hearings, my belief that any situation, given the right circumstances, can improve, was validated by the testimony of Dr. Gerald Fischbach, the director of the National Institute of Neurological Disorders and Stroke (part of the NIH). Dr. Fischbach postulated that with sufficient funding, scientists might be able to cure Parkinson's disease in five to ten years. If one of the congressional cameras had me in an isolated close-up, I'm sure I executed one of the finest double-takes of my career. I'd expected Fischbach to express confidence and lay down a challenge for researchers to match it and for Congress to support them in any way possible, but I wasn't expecting him to suggest a timeline. His testimony energized me. This was doable. I had been given the idea that a cure was possible, and I needed to act upon it.

I realized that I was ridiculously unqualified to contribute to this effort in any substantive way; I wasn't an MBA or a PhD—although a few years earlier, I had earned my GED. But my optimism had crystallized into definitive hope. And over the course of the next year, that hope became the inspiration for a streamlined private foundation, one that could galvanize the patient community and set up its own infrastructure to raise significant money, identify underfunded scientists, and provide the support they needed as quickly as possible.

Ironic that in order to do my life's work, I had to quit my day job.

Permanent Vacation

PEYPIN D'AIGUES, PROVENCE, FRANCE

JULY 2000

In a gravel parking lot in the Provençal village of Peypin d'Aigues, I leaned against a plane tree and observed with the same respectful fascination something as timeless as the sea turtle I'd seen off the coast of St. John's the previous winter: two elderly Frenchmen in rumpled white linen playing a game of *boules*. It seemed more a dance than a game, and their conversation had a guttural musical quality to it. After one contentious exchange, apparently having to do with the legal point of release, they sauntered a few steps to a weathered bench, retrieved a pair of wine goblets, and in the time it took for each to take a sip, forgot about their dispute. I took a swig from the tall bottle of water I had been nursing since arriving at the airport in Marseille. Sam was back in the States (he didn't want to miss summer camp), and our twins Schuyler and Aquinnah, five years old at the time, were asleep in the car. Tracy stepped into the real estate office to meet our contact, while our friend Iwa tipped the driver who had delivered us this far, just a kilometer or so away from the villa we had rented for the next two weeks. The *agent de biens immobiliers* would drive us the rest of the way.

It had been a long trip, and I had no idea what to expect from the place. But as we negotiated the long driveway up to the villa, my concerns vanished. Rounding one last bend in the approach allowed for a full reveal: there stood a sprawling, custard-colored mansard confection with red-clay tiles, turrets, and a windmill, floating in a sea of lavender. I couldn't have asked for a better place to reflect upon the transformative events of the first half of the year and to ponder the possibilities of the next.

My last few months as Mike Flaherty had been emotional, exhausting, and bittersweet. But aside from my concerns for the cast and crew, whose livelihoods would be affected, at least in the short term, I had no regrets. But neither did I have any real plans. The wind-down to the final episode coincided with an inchoate desire to start something like a foundation (though I had no idea what that meant). The love, support, and encouragement I was receiving from friends, family, and quite literally countless people around the world was carrying me forward through this transition. It did occur to me that this might be an appropriate time to attempt a memoir. The effort would, I reasoned, provide an opportunity for reflection and perspective and allow me to convey my gratitude for all the circumstances in my life—good and bad. I also figured that if the book made any money, I could put it toward PD research.

Realistically though, my life after this trip to France was as blank as the pages in the book I had yet to write. Beyond this period of rest lay the rest of my life, and it was nothing but undedicated time and space. I wasn't setting off on a holiday; I was embarking on an odyssey that would no doubt last longer than these two weeks away from New York. For my family, this was a vacation; for me, it was an invocation. I was looking for a sign or an omen—and I was willing to pay in francs. Little did I know that within that French fortnight, I would be visited by a muse, and in truly Homeric fashion, it would take the form of a lone rider descending from the mountaintop— sort of.

Provence was like a dream. The moment and setting inspired me to pause and appreciate how blessed my life had been. After all, there I was, this army brat from Canada, and for two weeks my family and I had the run of a centuries-old French villa.

Photos of the owners' family, mostly shots of their young children, festooned the villa's walls. Genevieve, the cook and housekeeper, who was good-natured and gracious but spoke no English, would point proudly at the portraits of the little girls and exclaim, *"Princesse! Princesse!"* We wrote this off as a simple expression of affection for her young charges, until we began noticing more photographs of elegant people in regal settings and found linens in the closet emblazoned with elaborate coats of arms and, finally, a piece of personalized stationery identifying the master of the household as the heir to the throne of a European principality. I couldn't stop giggling. This was some serious line-jumping.

While the kids splashed in the aggressively unheated pool, Jean-Luc, Genevieve's husband, served as my guide on daily treks through the surrounding hillside. Quite a naturalist, he constantly scanned the skies in hopes of sighting one of the many young eagles hatched that spring from the local aeries.

"Michel!" he'd exclaim, pointing repeatedly at the horizon or directly above his head. *"Regarde, regarde! Aigle, aigle!"*

I'd steal a quick peek skyward, but not without some trepidation. On the first of these hikes, Jean-Luc had warned me that in addition to the eagles, the local fauna also featured a healthy population of feral pigs—wild boar—or as Jean-Luc would say, *"cochons savage."* Nasty, two-hundred-pound bristle-brush battering rams; without warning, they could charge out of the underbrush and eviscerate you with eight-inch tusks. They don't even need a reason.

"Yeah, I see the eagle, Jean-Luc . . . No, I don't need the binoculars, *merci* anyway."

For her part, Tracy had discovered a bicycle collection in a shed behind the villa, which Jean-Luc kept in good repair and made available to us. My wife is an enthusiastic cyclist, so she was thrilled at the chance to ride down, into, up, and out of the valleys and villages surrounding our villa. She even convinced me to ride along, although after two or three of the grueling local hills, being gutted by a wild pig seemed preferable.

What little television we'd been watching since we arrived in Provence had included coverage of the spectacular Tour de France. The annual event, France's greatest sporting tradition, had been sweeping through the mountains and villages in the country, and the heroics of the athletes, especially American Lance Armstrong, had inspired Tracy. I too had been following Lance's progress, but for different reasons.

On one of our last days in Provence, we learned that the next stage of the Tour would race through the nearby town of Pertuis. We woke early, had an amazing *fromage* and baguette breakfast on the terrace, and set off for the village. After an hour or so of waiting for the cyclists, during which we soaked up the ambiance and local color, letting the kids eat ice cream after ice cream from a nearby vendor's cart, a buzz began to build in the crowd. We could feel the pavement beneath our feet begin to vibrate. The spectators pressed toward the street for a better view. From what I had seen of these events on television, it always seemed that the crowd ventured a little too close to the cyclists, and it surprised me that there weren't more disasters along the route. Tracy and I each grabbed a twin by the hand and held fast as the pack zoomed by. It was hard to distinguish one bike from another; they became a single elongated metallic blur. The rainbow palette of their team jerseys and the gleaming chrome of their bicycles *did* draw you in like a magnet. We thought that day in Pertuis was as up-close-and-personal a Tour de France encounter as we could hope for. But we didn't know what awaited us in Paris.

In spite of one particularly unsavory period in its history when it served as the World War II headquarters for the occupying Nazis, we loved the Hôtel de Crillon. The floor-to-ceiling windows in our rooms overlooked the Place de la Concorde, offering clear views of the Tuileries Gardens, the Musée de l'Orangerie, and, across the Seine, the Palais Bourbon.

Shortly after checking in, I placed a call to our friend Philippe de Boeuf, the hotel manager. "Why," as I had noticed when we pulled up in front of the hotel, "is the state flag of Texas flying above the hotel?"

"It's for Lance Armstrong," he said in his Charles Boyer accent. "He's in town for the Tour de France. Tomorrow's the last stage, and the Crillon is his home when he's in Paris."

In addition to our high regard for Lance's accomplishments as history's greatest competitive cyclist, both Tracy and I had been inspired, like so many others around the world, by his courage and perseverance in overcoming the challenge of testicular cancer that threatened not only his career, but his life as well. He had become a hero to many stricken with cancer. I was especially impressed by his strength in facing his own ordeal and his recognition of the situation faced by others. The Lance Armstrong Foundation, although still relatively young, was already living up to its mission statement: "To inspire and empower cancer sufferers and their families under the motto 'unity is strength, knowledge is power, and attitude is everything.'"

I considered Lance, along with Christopher Reeve, a role model for what I hoped to accomplish. These were both men who had met transforming challenges. Each had taken a negative and turned it into a positive. I didn't have to let the terms of a disease define me—I could redefine the terms. And maybe in the process get a better deal for me and everyone else in my situation.

"It's funny you should mention the flag," Philippe continued. "Lance's wife, Kristin, just saw you and your family in the lobby, and she and Lance wish to invite you to a reception in the hotel this afternoon."

I didn't have to give it much thought, or even check with Tracy.

Before I let Philippe off the phone, I had a request. A day or two before we left Provence, we'd received a call from the States informing us that we'd each been nominated for Emmy awards—me for the last season of *Spin City,* and Tracy for a guest role on an episode of *Law & Order SVU.* While Tracy was in the twins' room, helping them unpack, I asked Philippe if it would be possible for the hotel's patisserie chef to create a cake for Tracy in the shape of an Emmy. Of course, this required explaining what the hell an Emmy was, and what it looked like. Less a tribute to my powers of description than to the chef's culinary artistry, the Emmy-shaped chocolate creation would later prove to be both incredibly accurate and completely delicious.

Jarring as it was to see the Texas flag over the Hôtel de Crillon, to be in a room full of people in Paris speaking with a Texas twang also took some getting used to—"I'm fixin' to have me some of that there pâté." At least two people were having a conversation in French—Tracy and Lance's wife, Kristin. Tracy has always had a fantasy of living in France, immersing herself in the culture and the language. I didn't actively discourage the idea; I wouldn't have minded living in Provence for a month or however long it took for me to learn to say, "I've been attacked by a wild boar. Help me find my spleen!" Schuyler and Aquinnah, meanwhile, were proving my theory that when introduced into a room full of adults, children are instinctively drawn to any human tinier than they are; they immediately began fussing over Lance and Kristin's year-old son, Luke.

I was happily surprised to run into an old friend among the Texans—Robin Williams. A fanatical cyclist, logging hundreds of miles a week on the highways and byways around the San Francisco Bay area, Robin had a long-standing mutual admiration society with Lance. They'd ride together often, and Robin even had some of his bikes shipped to Paris so he could join Lance on practice runs.

Lance made a brief appearance. He was, after all, still in the middle of the race. I've never met a fitter human being—so athletically trim, he could cut paper. His famously handsome features, all angles with bright engaging eyes, betrayed none of the intense fatigue he surely felt having reached the final stage of the world's most punishing endurance test. I told him that since we'd arrived in France, we'd been following his

progress, but were sorry that we'd miss the end of the race—
our plans had us flying back to New York on the Concorde
Sunday morning. Lance quickly talked us out of that plan, in-
viting us not only to stay and watch the race with his family
from the grandstand on the Champs-Elysées, but also to attend Sunday night's victory celebration at the Musée d'Orsay.

Luckily our travel agent found and booked seats for us on
the Monday flight. For a while it had looked like we might
have to stay until Tuesday. Oh well, we thought, even if we
didn't find seats on the Monday flight, leaving on Tuesday's
Concorde wouldn't be the worst thing in the world. Actually,
as it happened, it might have been—but I'll get to that.

PARIS, FRANCE · SUNDAY, JULY 23, 2000

Sunny summer mornings in Paris are always a gift, but even
in that context, this day was exceptional. The section of the
grandstand reserved for the Armstrong family was on the
Champs-Elysées, just steps away from the Place de la Concorde. We were positioned right next to the finish line, close
enough to the action to be cooled by the almost violent displacement of air created as the peloton roared past us with
each lap. Naturally, a supportive chorus of cheers arose among
our group when Lance's yellow jersey sped by. But then, all of
Paris seemed to be cheering for the phenomenal young American. As if the blurring whoosh of passing racers weren't
enough, we were further entertained by the hysterical color
commentary of Robin Williams and his friend, Monty Python legend Eric Idle, who had flown in for the day.

Robin Williams is always "on," unleashing his rapid-fire, stream-of-consciousness patter on anyone who is lucky enough to be within the sound of his voice or even his line of vision; and you don't have to "get it" to find him excruciatingly funny. The twins, all of five years old, were enthralled by this giant ten-year-old boy whom they alternately described as "funny" and "scary." Robin, rabid cycling fan that he is, was especially thrilled to be so close to the action, or as he later described the experience to the *New Yorker,* "right in the middle of the big *mishpocha* . . . It gave you a kick in the heart." And it only got better.

Just after the pack zoomed by on their penultimate circuit of the course, Robin, Eric, and I were approached with a once-in-a-lifetime offer. Did we want to ride in the official Renault pace car as it led the peloton for the bell lap on the Champs-Elysées? I might have said *"Oui,"* or maybe it was "Whee!," but either way, I managed to squeak out some sort of affirmative response.

Whenever I am blessed by an opportunity such as this, my feeling of gratitude reminds me of just how many extraordinary opportunities I've been presented with in my life. I've played hockey with Bobby Orr on the ice at Boston Garden; I sat with Princess Diana at the royal London premiere of *Back to the Future;* I have, on separate occasions, played guitar, however badly, onstage with Bruce Springsteen, Elvis Costello, Sting, Elton John, Billy Joel, James Taylor, Levon Helm, John Mayer, and Aerosmith; and I have eaten dinner at the White House and sat with Nancy Pelosi in her office during the minutes leading up to her appearance as the first female speaker of the house to preside over a State of the Union Address. I'm sure there are many other *Forrest Gump* moments that I'm forgetting. I don't mention them as boasts, but rather as evidence of how ridiculously lucky I have been to have lived the life that I have. The ride I was about to go on easily served as a metaphor for the ride I'd been on before and have been on since.

As well as being one of the kindest and funniest people I've ever spent any amount of time with, Robin Williams is also (I'm not being indiscreet here—he's kind of famous for it) the sweatiest. He's one of those guys that is so hirsute, patting him on the back feels like you're fluffing a down comforter—and if it's a warm day, a *wet* down comforter. Seconds after we climbed into the pace car, the temperature in the car jumped precipitously as it absorbed the extra heat emanating from the *schvitzing* Mr. Williams. But soon we were well up to speed, and the breeze dried the beads of sweat on our faces and cooled the backs of our necks as we craned around to see the action.

It's awesome enough when this thundering herd of men and machines streaks past you as you remain static at a barely safe distance on the side of the road, but to witness it coming at you head-on, full speed, protected only by a fluctuating distance beyond your control—it's a complete rush. It was easy to distinguish Lance and his teammates from their competitors. Lance, of course, was wearing the leader's yellow jersey, but I was both shocked and impressed that he and his teammates were stealing sips as they rode, not from water bottles, but from crystal flutes of champagne. Lance later explained that on the last lap, "the winning team hands out champagne to the other coaches as a show of respect," adding somewhat unconvincingly, "you fake that sip."

Lance and the U.S. Postal Team went into the day all but assured of victory. He knew when I spoke to him the day before that his second consecutive Tour de France win was *dans le sac,* but added, "The last stage is still official. It looks pretty ceremonial, but if you're leading by seven minutes and fall over a hundred feet before the finish line and can't finish, you don't win." From where Eric, Robin, and I were sitting—and no three people had better seats—an entire magnum of champagne could not have prevented his advance to the victory stand. By the way, the view out the front of the car was impressive in its own right. Speeding up a completely empty Champs-Elysées, flanked by teeming crowds of frenzied Parisians, had all of us in the car speechless—well, almost speechless. Along one stretch of the route, as we approached one of Paris's most iconic landmarks, Robin managed to blurt out, "Not since Hitler has anyone had this view of the Arc de Triomphe."

To this day, whenever I run into Robin or Eric, the first words we exchange are usually "We'll always have Paris." As lengthy as my list of *Through the Looking-Glass* adventures may be, I'm sure that, given the lives and careers of my two companions, theirs are even longer and more sensational. But it was clear that not one of us was too jaded to be reduced to giggles. This day was special, "like waiting outside Yankee Stadium and suddenly finding Joe DiMaggio," according to Robin.

Exiting the car to join the Armstrong family (as well as my own—including a visibly envious Tracy) for the awards presentation, I wondered aloud whom I should speak to about having everybody do one more lap so I could take pictures this time.

At the hotel that evening, as Tracy and I dressed for the victory celebration at the Musée d'Orsay, Schuyler asked me about the book I planned to write. "What's it about?"

Good question. "Well," I said, "I guess it's about me."

"What about you?" Aquinnah asked. "About you being a dad?"

"Oh," Schuyler said. "About you being 'Shaky Dad.'"

"Yeah," I said, impressed by her perception.

Aquinnah wanted a fuller picture. "But Shaky Dad doing what? Riding a bicycle?"

Tracy, laughing now, looked at me to see how far I was going to let this go.

"Yeah, that's it," I said. "Shaky Dad riding a bicycle. Something like that."

As we arrived at the Musée d'Orsay later that night, the onetime railway station and current art museum was bathed in a fairy-tale glow. Even in the electric age, Paris at night still appears to be lit purely by gaslight, greasy smears of luminescence, a million candles flickering in syncopation from inside hand-blown glass jars. At first the museum seemed like an odd venue for this party. After all, these were athletes, jocks, and they had just won the Super Bowl of bike racing. Not just won; they kicked ass. I mean, it's not that I was expecting a kegger, but this all seemed a bit refined. In America, I could imagine the whole team at Scores thumb-spraying shaken bottles of cheap champagne all over the pole dancers, instead of here, washing down canapés with Cristal against the backdrop of *Whistler's Mother*. The celebration added to my gathering impression of how the French view of sport differs from our own. Obviously they are not immune to the taint of commercial excess, rampant cheating, and egos inflated in proportion to salaries, but as much as they celebrate any particular athlete, their deepest reverence is for sport itself. Regardless of the fact that Lance and his team had won before and would win many more times in the years ahead, the elegance of the evening made clear that a victory in the Tour de France was a moment to be savored.

Tracy and I spent much of the evening with Lance's mom, Linda. When you ask Lance about the source of his optimism, right away he talks about his mother: "We didn't have money or the opportunities that others did. But she never complained. If I did complain about something, my mom was always there to say, 'Tomorrow is a new day.' Optimism has always been a way of life for us."

The celebration included a large contingent of cancer patients, some survivors, some still struggling through treatment. I learned that their presence was a constant at events such as this. Lance explained, "That has been a real motivating factor for me throughout my career, to see people in the same situation who understand that I'm riding not just to win a bike race, but for a whole other set of reasons." Tracy and I had been so taken by how generously he shared that spirit. A man capable of seemingly superhuman accomplishments, he was all the more admirable because of his vulnerability and his willingness to make that as much a part of his identity as his strength.

Later, before returning to the Crillon, Tracy and I sought out Lance to thank him not only for talking us into sticking around for the race, but for including us in the celebration as well. I had so many questions about all the people I had met that night, particularly those with a connection to his foundation. How had he woven together this fabric of support? How hands-on was his leadership, and how had he managed to cultivate a culture within the organization that was so true to his spirit of courage, hope, and accomplishment? We made plans to meet after the summer in New York, so I could learn more about his work with the foundation.

My mini Gallic Odyssey—much better than the epic version because I got to bring my family along—seemed to have served a greater purpose than just two weeks of R & R. My invocation had been answered. Lance had ridden down from the mountains with what might be at the very least a partial map for the next leg of my journey.

CHARLES DE GAULLE AIRPORT, PARIS, FRANCE
JULY 24, 2000

There was no experience quite like flying on the Concorde. It was ridiculously expensive, and as soon as you were on board, you realized that you weren't paying that premium for leg, head, or seat space. The appointments were as deluxe as possible, given the constraints of the plane's narrow tubular shape. Obviously, the big attraction and the big-ticket price had to do with the time savings—Paris to New York in three hours. Years earlier, I once awoke in London, had breakfast, took the Concorde to New York, transferred to an American Airlines flight to Los Angeles, and was at work on the set of

Family Ties by 1:00 that afternoon. With a nod to time zones, it's still a testament to the miracle of the Concorde.

At least the waiting area at the Charles de Gaulle Airport offered plenty of room to spread out. On that Monday morning after the Tour de France, my family was taking advantage of every inch. The girls were running amok, which at five years old was basically their job description. Our friend Iwa kept an eye on the kids and double-checked with the attendant at the desk that our bags were all properly processed. I was busy talking to Tracy, and Tracy was busy freaking out— not that anyone else would have noticed, but I know when she's rattled, like she knows when I'm bullshitting. Since I had known her, Tracy had come a long way in overcoming her fear of flying. Which is a good thing, because as a young family, we were constantly on the move, whether for work or recreation. Perhaps it seemed too frail and flimsy to fly so far so fast, but there was something about the Concorde that particularly unnerved Tracy. Today was no exception. I was doing my best to be patient. Flying never bothered me anyway, but I had always felt especially safe on the Concorde, particularly the Air France Concorde. I had no evidentiary support for this bias. It just seemed to me that the French ran a pretty efficient operation, and so naturally, they kept their SSTs in good working order. I floated this theory to Tracy, but she was not impressed. At a loss, I recommended a Valium.

"Now that," she said, "makes sense."

"I promise you, T," I said, handing her a glass of water to go with her pill, "if it scares you this much, this will be the last time we'll ever fly on the Concorde."

The trip was smooth and anxiety-free and, as advertised, was approximately three hours from takeoff to touchdown at JFK. At about the same time the next day, Tuesday, July 25, I sat in my Manhattan office with the television on, sorting through the mail that had accumulated while we were away. A graphic on the TV screen announced a breaking news bulletin. As the images rolled, whatever mail I was holding in my hands floated to the carpet. The video, so graphic, so horrific, was all the sensory input I could process. I was deaf to the accompanying audio. The Air France Concorde, either in an attempted landing or aborted take-off—I couldn't tell—slammed into the earth, disintegrating into a maelstrom of red flame and black smoke. They re-racked the video, and this time I took in the tragic details. "At approximately five P.M. local time, a New York–bound Concorde jet crashed in a ball of fire shortly after taking off from Paris, killing 113 people."

Sometimes, when you're alone, minutes pass before you even realize you're crying.

NEW YORK CITY · SEPTEMBER 2000

Lance made good on his promise, and come September, we met at my production company offices in New York to discuss foundation building. Accompanying Lance were Howard Chalmers, the president of the Lance Armstrong Foundation, and Jeffrey Garvey, its chairman, both of whom I had met in Paris. Lance recalled that in 1997, he'd sat around a table at a Mexican restaurant in Austin with a few friends and associates and begun dreaming about what their foundation might accomplish. Amazingly, Lance was starting something he couldn't be sure he'd be around to see completed. By that time, Lance's testicular cancer had spread to his abdomen, lungs, and brain, and the treatments were no guarantee of recovery or even survival. Now in 2000, with the disease in remission, he had two Tour de France yellow jerseys in his closet and had already raised millions for cancer-related efforts.

Obviously Lance gave the foundation more than a name and a face. He imbued it with his attitude and his passion for winning. "You know, it's not like we have good news every day in this fight. But we're in it, we're motivated, and ultimately we think we can make a difference."

In addition to the nuts and bolts—the day-to-day business aspects that go into running a 501(c)(3)—Lance explained what it meant to have his name on the foundation's door, outlining the manner in which his profile provided leverage on behalf of those his foundation was trying to help. We also spoke about the stigmas attached to both Parkinson's and cancer, and how important it was for those that were able to speak up to do so. "I was a young man and I had testicular cancer. You can imagine the shit people were saying. They still say it to this day. I don't care. I don't let that stuff affect me."

I was already motivated, but Lance managed to get me even more fired up.

On a practical level, I asked him what he thought was the essential ingredient for a successful foundation. "It's all about the people you surround yourself with," he said. "You can't do it alone."

Strangely Familiar

In June of 1989, just days after Sam was born, my mom and dad made the trip down from Canada to check him out. Maybe Dad knew it would be one of his few opportunities to cradle his newest grandson in his ursine embrace—he'd be gone by January—because he didn't want to let Sam go. Mom had to wrestle the kid away from his gramps.

One morning as we sat by the pool, Mom, patting Sam to sleep on her shoulder in the dappled California sunlight, offered this prediction: "Some of the best friends you'll ever meet in your life, you'll meet through your children—mothers and fathers of their friends, parents from school. You'll see. That's the way it was for Bill and me. It's one of the many gifts of parenting."

As Sam progressed through childhood, he introduced us, one way or another, to lots of new friends, a handful of whom are now among our closest. When the twins, Aquinnah and Schuyler, came along, our circle of friends grew wider. I had long accepted my mother's prediction as the purest form of wisdom, but even Mom couldn't have foreseen the phenomenon I would encounter when the girls entered preschool.

After the first few times I met Curtis Schenker, my instinct was not to invite him into our circle, but to file for a restraining order.

Throughout my life, I've set some lofty goals for myself. In each case, to varying degrees, my pursuit of the desired outcome has been fueled by ambition, hope, arrogance, and youthful (sometimes not-so-youthful) foolishness. Every failure I have considered my own, but every success has been shared. I can always come up with a list of people who have had something to do with what went right. It was that way with my career—Gary Goldberg, Bob Zemeckis, Steven Spielberg, the actors I worked with, and of course, the audiences who kept me in business—and also with my family—Tracy, Tracy, and Tracy. It's impossible to imagine, however, how the foundation's story would have unfolded were it not for the early, ongoing, and irrepressibly optimistic contributions of a single hedge fund manager, who had absolutely no previous connection to Parkinson's.

From the moment we met her, we absolutely loved Curtis Schenker's daughter, Ally. She was a bright and adorable giggle machine, and her temperament, interests, and physical appearance were so similar to our girls that Tracy and I dubbed her "the third twin." The three of them were tight as ticks. Carolyn, Curtis's wife and Ally's mother, seemed to be the antithesis of the cliché Upper East Side socialite mom. Her gracious humor, sense of perspective, and kind nature immediately appealed to Tracy, and their friendship soon expanded beyond the boundaries of the small talk accompanying preschool drop-off and pick-up.

Meanwhile, Ally had become an after-school and weekend playdate fixture at our apartment, and I'd spoken with Carolyn on a few occasions when I could break away from my *Spin City* schedule to handle pick-up or drop-off duty myself. It took quite a few parents' day visits, class outings, and potluck dinners before I associated either Ally or Carolyn with this wild-eyed, red-haired dad named Curtis. I knew he had to be the father of one of these kids, but I could have sworn the guy was stalking me. Perched on one of those tiny red plastic chairs at a preschool function, swishing the dregs of the apple juice in my Dixie cup, I'd turn, and he'd be next to me in his own little chair. I always had the sense that he began talking a minute or two before he had my attention and continued for at least a couple of minutes after he'd lost it.

Then there was the walk-on. That's when he got me. For their annual fund-raising gala, the 92nd Street Y preschool asks parents and friends of the Y to donate high-end goods, services, and experiences for auction. Walk-ons—non-speaking extra roles in movies or television series—are often big-ticket items at these things. It always struck me as funny that these well-heeled, accomplished, and sophisticated New Yorkers would dole out sometimes tens of thousands of dollars for the privilege of spending a day as an extra, or, to be PC, an "atmospheric artist." This is the ninth circle of show business hell with a boxed lunch. But hey, if it could raise money for a worthwhile purpose, I was always willing to offer a day at *Spin City*. So I did, and guess who bought it?

I called my wife from my dressing room at our Chelsea Piers soundstage. "Tracy, you won't believe who's here," I whispered urgently. Several thick walls and about five hundred yards of hallway separated me from anyone who could have overheard our conversation, but my sotto voce was more about labored oxygen intake than discretion. "I just went down to camera rehearsal, and that crazy red-haired guy from the Y was on the set."

"That's Curtis Schenker," Tracy said, "Ally's dad. You remember my friend, Carolyn."

"Curtis. Right—*crazy* Curtis."

"He is *not* crazy," Tracy countered. "He's just friendly. You'll actually like him. He's smart, he's funny, and he's generous. You wouldn't believe how much he bid to do this today. Be *nice* to him."

Back on the stage, we were setting the background, which means establishing the position and the movements of the nonspeaking cast that silently populates the shows we watch. Determined to be a quality host whatever my misgivings, I attached a smile to my face and walked over to the lucky auction winner.

"Curtis," I said, "this scene opens with a tracking shot of me. The camera is on a dolly, and it's going to roll back, lead me down the hallway, around this desk, and dump me off at the office door. Let's make sure you're in frame the whole time so that you're guaranteed to be a part of the shot."

I appreciated how into it he was—not jaded in any way. In fact, he had an odd charm. I put him front and center in the opening shot of the episode with forty seconds of uninterrupted screen time. He did a nice job too—relaxed, natural, didn't move like a stick of wood, and didn't lock eyes with the camera lens.

The next time I saw him, I told him he was going to love the episode. He called ten friends and told them to watch. But when we got the show into final editing, we were eight minutes long. Something had to go. That something, we decided, had to be the opening scene—Curtis's scene. Now, I've actually heard of situations in which someone has paid a generous price at auction for one of these walk-on film or TV roles, been cut out, and then filed suit. Luckily, Curtis didn't do that. Accepting my explanation and apology with understanding and even a sense of humor, he told me he would have written a check to the Y anyway. And after all, he had a good time. Curtis, it turned out, wasn't a crazy stalker, but actually a pretty decent guy.

On the surface, the two of us would seem to have little in common, apart from age. A product of the New York private school system, Curtis went on to graduate from Penn, did well on Wall Street, and then formed a successful hedge fund business, all before he was thirty years old. I bounced through a series of public schools in Canada, dropped out in the eleventh grade, then did well pretending to be a guy who wanted to work on Wall Street and invest in a few hedge funds. Soon the similarities became more apparent. We're both hapless rock star wannabes who can identify any song on satellite classic rock radio seconds before the artist's ID pops up; we're each completely undeserving of the amazing women we convinced to marry us; and we're both hard-core optimists.

NEW YORK CITY · MAY 31, 2000

In May of 2000, Curtis and Carolyn invited Tracy and me to the Robin Hood gala and auction in New York City. This annual event features a who's who of the New York financial community. Hedge fund managers, private equity investors, venture capitalists, bankers, bond traders, corporate CEOs, and real estate investors—this event assembled in one room, on one night, the heaviest of Wall Street's heavy hitters. Also in attendance were sports and showbiz celebrities, like Gwyneth Paltrow and basketball coach Pat Riley. Robin Williams served as emcee, and The Who provided the musical entertainment. With much of the world's private wealth represented in this single convention hall, though, the Wall Street titans were the real stars. You couldn't swing a millionaire without hitting a billionaire. I'm sure many of you, given today's economic crisis, would like to do just that. As we all know now, some of these supernovas would, in the not so distant future, fall crashing to the earth.

There could be no argument about the munificence on display that night, however (and as you'll see, whatever the present attitude toward the financial community, I can personally attest to their continuing generosity and general sense of social responsibility). Beneficiaries of the aptly named Robin Hood Foundation included a wide variety of groups and private agencies that served the city's underprivileged. Tracy and I were awestruck by the numbers flying around during the live auction—upward of a million dollars for some of the big-ticket items, like an executive jet passage to Egypt for a cruise down the Nile on a private yacht. Writing about this night in *Lucky Man*, I mentioned the perils of being a Parkinson's patient at such an auction. A poorly timed arm spasm could wipe out the kids' college educations. So to play it safe, I sat on my hands and tried to avoid stepping on my jawbone.

There was something different in the philanthropic air that night. This was not just patronage, it was participation; not just charity, but an investment in an outcome. In the days following, Curtis and I discussed the possibility of putting together a

Parkinson's research fund-raiser in New York. Curtis was certain that when the time was right, he could reach out to his friends and associates with a considerable degree of success.

Our Ms. Brooks

Almost unconsciously, I had been taking Lance's advice, assembling the parts of a machine capable of organizing, processing, and converting hope into an answer to Parkinson's. What I needed most was a partner, an executive director who could implement my vision.

"Find someone from Wall Street," Curtis advised. "The business model you're after is innovative, aggressive, and entrepreneurial—a start-up."

We contacted an executive search firm, specializing in the nonprofit sector. "But don't just look for candidates from traditional philanthropic organizations," we instructed. "Look to the private sector." The search firm thought we were nuts. How would we ever lure executives away from their big Wall Street salaries? By the beginning of October, my partner on *Spin City,* Nelle Fortenberry, and a few friends from the Parkinson's advocacy community had narrowed the field of several dozen candidates down to three finalists.

When the doors to the conference room opened, Debi Brooks strode in for her interview with an air of easy confidence, as though she knew she had what it takes, but was affable and humble enough to give us the time we needed to figure that out for ourselves. She was instantly engaging. It quickly became obvious that her greatest asset was her mind, with her heart a close second—precisely the combination required to captain a competitive nonprofit organization. I turned to Nelle and said, "So when exactly were you going to tell me about her?"

A former vice president in the Fixed Income and Asset Management Divisions at Goldman Sachs, Debi didn't view my assertion that a cure for Parkinson's was possible within a decade as simply the wishful thinking of the afflicted. I could already see, during those first few minutes of what has become one of the most lasting relationships of my life, that to Debi optimism and pragmatism were not oil and water. While the other candidates were certainly qualified and would no doubt have brought their own unique talents to the mission, it was obvious that Debi was the home run. By the end of the business day, she would be offered and have accepted the job; three days later, she was in the office—and we were off.

MJF FOUNDATION PLANNING MEETING,
NEW YORK CITY · OCTOBER 23, 2000

No sooner did I welcome Debi into the job than I laid down the conditions for her termination. "The last thing I want is for you and I to find ourselves discussing our twentieth annual fund-raiser. In fact, if that day ever comes, you're fired."

She laughed, but I knew she shared the underlying urgency. Our goal was nothing short of obsolescence. Ultimately that's also how I began my pitch to the group of advisors who convened at Dreamworks' corporate headquarters in New York: "I need you to help me go out of business."

Seated around the table were CEOs, entrepreneurs, and leaders of major companies—titans on the highest levels. And here I was, asking them to help me design a business that *wasn't* built to last: "If we can find a cure for Parkinson's, our work is done."

It could have been a scene out of *The Secret of My Success* or one of Alex Keaton's wet dreams—the young executive addressing his troops in a midtown high-rise boardroom. In fact, in my previous life, only when playing characters— Alex P. Keaton, Mike Flaherty, or some other young gogetter—did I wear a suit and tie. I certainly never went through that much trouble for studio executives or media interviews. But there I was in a navy blue suit, a red tie, and a blue button-down shirt.

Elaborating on the "getting into business to go out of business" theme with which I'd initiated this meeting, I indicated that it was my hope to build an organization fundamentally different from any that presently existed.

"We're not setting up a bank," I told them. "When money comes in, it will go back out immediately."

Debi seconded with, "We're not establishing an endowment. We're willing to spend every penny we take in."

This philosophy involves risk, anathema to most nonprofit corporations. To me, risk equals opportunity. Almost everyone in the room that day had a daily relationship with risk. In addition to hedge fund managers and financial types, there were executives from publishing and the entertainment industry—all of them understood that you can't win if you don't place a bet. As Debi put it, "We aren't here to play it safe, but to do whatever it takes to cure Parkinson's."

Now I knew how Ray Kinsella of *Field of Dreams* felt when he stepped onto his Iowa cornfield turned baseball diamond to find Shoeless Joe and the 1919 White Sox going through their warm-ups. Like Ray, I had heeded the advice of an internal voice: "If you build it, they will come."

I knew I didn't have to go in front of this group and ask, "*Can* we build it?" Instead, I could ask, "*How* do we build it?"

Within two weeks, the Michael J. Fox Foundation for Parkinson's Research would be granted our certificate of incorporation and our provisional 501(c)(3) nonprofit ID number. Less than a year earlier, I had stepped away from my acting career with no specific direction in mind. And now, here I was, stepping into an entirely new career—with a very specific direction, indeed.

Climbing Aboard

NEW YORK CITY · NOVEMBER 13, 2000

Two of Curtis's hedge fund colleagues, John Griffin and Glenn Dubin, whom we were hoping to recruit to our board of directors, recommended a "road show" event—Wall Street–style—to pitch our fledgling foundation to potential supporters. Curtis and Carolyn offered to host the gathering at their Park Avenue apartment and came up with a list of friends and associates. Affluent and philanthropic, these people get hit on every day by charities with a hand out and a story to tell. I don't go to a lot of cocktail parties, and like most people, I'm uncomfortable asking anyone for anything, but Curtis told me not to worry. "We'll probably need two hands for all the help we're going to get. It wouldn't hurt though," he suggested, "to invite a few people from showbiz." So I called some New York friends who had already shown us some love: Alan and Arlene Alda, Kevin Kline and Phoebe Cates, Billy Baldwin, Amy Irving, and Diane Sawyer.

Curtis spent the first hour of the party introducing me to the guests, and while walking me over to "potential difference-makers," he cocked his head and whispered a quick but detailed CV. With a scheduled 6:30 start, some guests came straight from work and were happy to loosen their Prada ties, toss back a drink, and chitchat about neurodegenerative disease. Oh—and eat piggies in blankets.

When it comes to cocktail parties, I realized a long time ago that I am all out of small talk. But on this night, and in this crowd, how could I not enjoy conversations like this one:

As I leaned against a door frame, cradling my Diet Coke, a gentleman in a dark suit jacket and blue jeans made his way across the room.

"Let me ask you something," he said to me. "How much do you guys think you'll raise this year?"

"Well, we're hoping for six million," I guessed. This was wildly optimistic, but that number had been tossed around.

"Six million?" A smile formed on the face of the man whom Curtis had introduced as Stevie. "I bet my wife, Alex, and I could raise that much money in one night."

It would turn out that Steven Cohen, hedge fund billion-aire and legendary art collector (a stroll through Alex and Steve's home is like a one-stop visit to the Tate, the Met, MoMA, and the Guggenheim—and that's just the foyer), would be true to his word. One of our first board members, he was so excited by the science that he would attend board meetings accompanied by a biology expert.

The business portion of the evening began with a primer on PD from Dr. Bill Langston, the founder and CEO of the Parkinson's Institute and our new chief scientific advisor. A scientific lecture on the cause and effect of cell death in the *substantia nigra* is indeed a strange way to kick off a Park Ave-nue cocktail party, but Dr. Bill made a compelling presenta-tion.

When it came time for me to address the crowd, Alan Alda introduced me. A good friend for many years, Alan is not only funny but also smart, incredibly well informed in matters of science, and genuine in his excitement about the prospects of research. To gain a better sense of the room and a fuller view of the crowd, I stepped up onto the marble fire-place hearth. My plan was to stick to the matter at hand and not to delve into politics, but this was November 13, 2000, one week after the presidential election, and we still didn't know whether George Bush or Al Gore would be the next President. The outcome would have a major impact on re-search science.

I started with a lame joke about "hanging chads" and then got down to business: private funding for PD research and what we could do to act upon scientific optimism about a potential cure. Emphasizing that when it came to a cure for Parkinson's, the question was not "if" but "when," I asked for their support. I was not just interested in a "write a check and hope for the best" version of philanthropy as usual, but an investment in a new kind of undertaking—the promise of quick action, accountability, innovation, and a positive outcome for which they could claim a share of responsibility.

Along with many of the CEOs from our inaugural planning meeting and several colleagues from my TV business, ten of the cocktail party attendees joined our board of directors. They would all be instrumental in the work ahead. Debi quickly began assembling a foundation staff, and within two weeks, the board approved the funding for our first research applications.

Out of the proceeds from *Lucky Man* and generous early gifts, we set aside one million dollars for this inaugural research initiative. Applications from researchers were due February 1, 2001, a remarkable six-week turnaround compared to the standard set by the NIH, which typically spends a year reviewing applications. For this reason, we dubbed our first research grants "Fast Track." Debi Brooks and Dr. Langston seemed a bit bold in their prediction that we would receive somewhere close to fifty applications, but when the deadline for applications closed, two hundred replies to the RFA had come in, from researchers based in twenty different countries: the total amount of research dollars requested surpassed twenty million dollars.

The science was ahead of the money, but we were officially in the race.

Rope-a-Dopamine

"I wish people would love everybody else the way
they love me. It would be a better world."

—MUHAMMAD ALI

I had forgotten all about the Johnny Wakelin song "Black Superman,"
with its lurching reggae rhythm and singsongy, pre-hip-hop rapping
pattern. But hearing it again through tiny earbud headphones that
didn't even exist at the time of its recording took me back. As a child of
the sixties and seventies, I understood that I shared the earth with gi-
ants. Some were socially and politically important figures—JFK, MLK,
RFK. Others were cultural icons like Elvis, the Beatles, Dylan, and the
Rolling Stones. There were heroes from the world of sports, and being a
typical Canadian rink-rat, most of mine played hockey—Gordie Howe,
Bobby Hull, and the best of the best before anyone had heard of Wayne
Gretzky, Bobby Orr. Over the course of my lifetime, however, one figure
had an impact in all of these realms—the most famous man on the
planet. An athlete, activist, advocate—some would say artist, and others anarchist—he was an African-American kid from Kentucky who,
incensed when another kid stole his bicycle, took up boxing. He went
on to change the sport, change his religion and his name, and, by
changing a lot of people's minds about war, change the world. When he
declared himself "The Greatest," he didn't say the greatest boxer, athlete, or horse's ass for that matter—he didn't care. He supplied the ad-
jective; selecting the appropriate noun was your business. He just said,
"The Greatest of All Time." And I agreed.

THE ARIZONA BILTMORE, PHOENIX

MARCH 18, 2001

I had been listening to "Black Superman" on this new MP3 player belonging to Howard Bingham, Muhammad Ali's personal photographer for more than forty years. Anywhere the champ goes, Howard is there, documenting the moment on film or just lightening the mood by providing a running off-color commentary in his manageable but distinctive blinking stutter. Sitting across the table from Howard in this Phoenix, Arizona, hotel suite, I could see Ali, sitting on the sofa, silhouetted against the picture window. I still couldn't believe it.

In town for "Fight Night," an annual fund-raiser for the Muhammad Ali Parkinson's Center, we were in my room waiting for Debi Brooks and an Ali Center volunteer to collect and shuttle us to a hotel conference room to shoot a Michael J. Fox Foundation public service announcement together. Even at that time, eight years ago, it was difficult for Muhammad to carry on an extended conversation. But he was alert, engaging, and the twinkle in his eye alone could have you laughing at what he didn't just say.

Then there was that magic trick—the flash of an empty hand, a clenched fist, a reach with the other hand, and presto, a scarf that wasn't there a moment ago appears. In the short time that I had been with him that day, he had already entertained me with this bit of prestidigitation a dozen times. If by the fourth or fifth time you haven't realized he is wearing a false thumb and concealing the scrunched up piece of cloth beneath it, he'll spill the secret himself. Ali's wife, Lonnie, told me later, "In the end he always tells people how he does it. He doesn't want to deceive them." Like all of his shtick, he managed to turn this endless repetition into something more like reinvention. It was somehow different every time, and you felt it a special privilege to be his audience.

A knock came at the door. Bingham collected his cameras and fired off a couple of shots as Ali and I exited the building and climbed into a waiting golf cart. The driver hadn't even turned over the electric motor yet when people in the parking lot started to realize that this lumbering giant, who had suddenly appeared close enough to cast a shadow on their golf shoes, was Muhammad Ali. As we drove away, we could hear the clatter of spikes sparking on asphalt as they jogged after the cart. We crossed a more populated courtyard area, and it became clear that the champ was out of the bag. A ripple of recognition spread across each face. I don't know how people had the time to react and then turn to tell a neighbor. Everybody just knew—the collective unconscious at work. And then we were swamped. But I in no way felt threatened. For one thing, the response was purely a loving one, and for another, it had absolutely nothing to do with me.

In the company of Muhammad Ali, you're not merely anonymous, you're invisible; but you don't mind because you're witnessing something extraordinary.

Courtesy of YouTube, I can reach back across those eight years and pull up the video that Muhammad and I shot that day. Artfully done in both black and white and color with a handheld camera, the tone was relaxed and conversational and (this has to be a first for a TV spot about neurodegenerative disease) even funny.

> Michael
>
> I'm five-foot-five, 130 pounds. He's six-foot-two, 255. We may look a little different. But we're actually very similar. We're both determined. We're both opinionated. And we both have Parkinson's. There's a lot of people out there just like us, and they need your help. So call the number below and get in our corner. You know, together we can win this fight.
>
> THE VIDEO CUTS TO A WHITE TITLE CARD WITH THE FOUNDATION'S CONTACT INFORMATION. THE INFORMATION IS READ ALOUD BY MEREDITH BAXTER (my old mom from *Family Ties*). CUT BACK TO THE SHOT OF MUHAMMAD AND ME, SIDE BY SIDE.
>
> Muhammad
>
> Five-foot-five? You wish.

As I watched the clip on the Internet, Nelle popped inside my office door to watch along with me. She remembered the day, of course, having helped to come up with the concept and produce the campaign with our friends at McCann-Erickson.

"Wow," she said, just after Muhammad had uttered the punch line (no pun intended). "He hasn't spoken that clearly in a long time."

"And I haven't seen myself that still on camera in a long time," I added. *And neither of us is any younger, and the fight goes on.*

PHILADELPHIA · AUGUST 2, 2000

A few months after the foundation's launch, we made two significant additions to our board. One was Donna Shalala, president of the University of Miami and erstwhile secretary of health and human services in the Clinton administration. Though Donna had no personal connection to Parkinson's disease, she obviously had tremendous insight into many of the issues we would be grappling with as a scientific foundation.

The second inductee was also a woman, formidable in her own right. Lonnie Ali's agreeing to serve on our board caused great excitement. Regardless of the attention I'd brought to Parkinson's, Muhammad Ali was far and away the world's most famous Parkinson's patient—Pope John Paul II at number two, and I, at best, a distant third. Obviously we were pleased by the endorsement that Lonnie's commitment represented. We valued her insight and experience as a caregiver—someone especially sensitive to the impact PD can have on a family, and the urgency with which we must pursue research.

I first spoke with Ali in 1998. "Muhammad was shocked when you went public," Lonnie told me. "He couldn't believe you had the guts to do that." Lonnie was there when he heard about my diagnosis. "I could tell by the expression on his face that he was thinking, Wow."

Ali called and left a message, but I was so flustered by the prospect of speaking to a true hero of mine that it took days to muster up the courage to call him back at his farm in Michigan. To ensure privacy and safeguard against interruption by any of my (at the time) three rambunctious children, I used the bathroom phone. It was a brief conversation. I sputtered something about being so honored to have the opportunity to talk to him. At first, his only response was breathing and a few tentative vocalizations. Closing my eyes, it was not difficult to summon up an image of Ali on the other end of the line. Then I heard a faint but steady whisper. "I'm sorry you have this, but with both of us in this fight, we're going to win now."

Nearly two years passed before we met face-to-face, or as Ali would surely point out, face-to-sternum. In August of 2000, I traveled to Philadelphia for the Republican National Convention, concerned about candidate George W. Bush's positions on federal funding of scientific research, particularly the exploration of embryonic stem cells. With plans already in the works to attend the Democratic Convention in Los Angeles, we saw Philadelphia as a chance to reach out, not only to those Repulicans who might impede our progress, but also to the substantial number of party loyalists, like Arlen Specter, Orrin Hatch, and John McCain, who supported our cause. Andrew Card, Bush's campaign manager and soon-to-be chief of staff, agreed to meet, as did a few conservative legislators. All in all, this was just a toe dip into the political currents. In just a few years, I'd wade up to my neck.

The surefire way to get attention at a political convention is to throw a party—the bigger, the splashier, and the more boldfaced names in attendance, the better. American shoe designer Kenneth Cole and *George* magazine co-sponsored an event in the Fox Foundation's honor that by all accounts was the party of all parties that week. Although right-leaning celebrities are rare, they were well-represented that evening, most notably by Arnold Schwarzenegger, former Terminator and future governor of California.

Being somewhat progressive in our politics, our group, including Tracy, did feel a bit like ducks in a desert. But we were ready to have a good time—whatever the political party, partying is apolitical. What I was most looking forward to that night was the appearance of a special guest at the party.

He almost didn't make it. Late summer storms rumbling across the Midwest and into parts of the East had Muhammad and his group rescheduling flights up to the very last minute. We waited at the hotel for word that he was on his way while, on the other side of Rittenhouse Square, the party had already begun. Hoping for one or two quiet minutes together before we left for the party, we resigned ourselves to being late. When the Alis arrived, they came up to our suite to say hello. My strongest memory was not of our handshake or hug, but of the elevator ride down to the lobby when this gentle giant produced a red satin scarf out of a fist full of thin air.

Like I said, it took four or five repeat performances at our next meeting until I understood the "how" of the trick, but I think I immediately sensed the "why." The enormous balled up fists no longer had the power to bring down a George Foreman in his prime, but they were still capable of a simple sleight of hand. A face that once broadcast a gamut of emotion, from wide-eyed, slack-jawed amazement at its own "prettiness," to the mask of a fierce warrior, was now frozen and without affect, save for the occasional subtle wink that signaled the end of the trick. And that voice that once sang and soared, offering both poetry and protest, now all but silenced, could still manage a paper-thin whisper: "One more time. Watch closer."

"I'm still magic," Ali seemed to be saying. "Pay no attention to the curtain in front of the man. I'm still in here. And I'm still the Greatest in the world."

When I meet people living with Parkinson's, rarely do I have knowledge of who and what they were before diagnosis. I relate to them in terms of our common difficulties in the here and now, and our shared optimism for an easier future. I don't know the totality of their loss or the incremental changes that marked the progression of their personal experience with Parkinson's—but they, of course, know mine. People have a strong sense of who I was long before I had PD and before they knew of my diagnosis. And their take on it will be as subjective as my own. When people first found out I had PD, I remember feeling uncomfortable that they might be inspired to rent old movies and watch reruns of *Spin City* in an effort to trace the accumulating effects of the disease. I'm sure many did.

When I see the old footage of my new friend, fighting, dancing, clowning, I do feel sad and angry for him. I wondered if he did too. Was it difficult for him to see a younger, healthier, and stronger version of Ali? When I mentioned this to Lonnie, she laughed. "Believe me, Muhammad's best afternoon is when he's watching himself," she said. "He amazes even himself. He'll be watching an old fight or an interview and he'll say, 'I was crazy, wasn't I?' He thanks God that there's footage of his life, so he can review it. He appreciates it. He's glad it's there."

Sometimes when channel surfing, I am ambushed by the image of a younger, healthier me. Usually, I just carry on clicking, giving it no more thought than I would an infomercial. There are times though, I confess, when I will pause and set the remote on the coffee table for a minute or two—sometimes longer.

PART TWO

Speaking Out

"Don't give up, don't lose hope, don't sell out."

—CHRISTOPHER REEVE

"Even a little dog can piss on a big building."

—JIM HIGHTOWER

Scott Olson/Getty Images

Talking the Walk and
Walking the Talk

If it's Monday, this must be Iowa, no wait, Iowa is this afternoon; if it's Monday morning, this must be Ohio. An odd feeling washes over me, as though I'm returning to a place I've never been before—Columbus, the real hometown of the fictional Alex P. Keaton.

Our flight is met by an eager and well-organized contingent from Congressman Sherrod Brown's surging campaign to move over to the U.S. Senate, specifically in the seat held by Repulican incumbent Mike DeWine. One member of the welcoming party, a big, cheerful, ex-cop-looking guy, introduces himself as our driver and has the requisite rented minivan to prove it. Over the last week, I've shaken hands and swapped stories with so many friendly volunteers in various Senate, House, and gubernatorial races around the country that I'm predisposed to like Sherrod's posse on general principle. Chronically undermanned and overworked, a loyal staff will battle tirelessly for a candidate they feel represents a promising future—and a reasonable shot at winning. True believers tell me they'll put in more effort and longer hours on campaign duty than at their regular full-time jobs and careers. I'm convinced that volunteer political staffers are a paradigm for the current theory embraced and promoted by high-priced corporate consultants, that optimism is a force-multiplier. As for our ex-cop driver, he delivers us to the campus of Ohio State University at 10:47 A.M., well in time for our 11:15 event. I may need every last one of those 1,680 seconds.

The weather in Ohio is like the weather in New York this October, unseasonably warm; the imperfect complement to a fresh set of tremors I'm trying to quell before the Brown rally. This sweating and trembling might confirm impressions of me as a wet-behind-the-ears political neophyte, but it raises scant notice from the minivan passenger next to me. John Rogers isn't oblivious to my PD symptoms so much as inured to them. When I first met this DC political trouble-shooter, he'd already put together a long and remarkable record of advocacy for Parkinson's disease, an avocation dedicated to a father and grandmother lost to Parkinson's. In his mid-forties, John is cautious but enthusiastic, with an intuitive sense of timing and the kind of smarts that keep him up at night. A crop of red hair, a desperately new goatee, a RAZR phone pressed to one ear, and a free hand pressed to the other, frame a warm, bespectacled, "Don't-I-know-you-from-high-school" face. Snapping shut the Motorola, he turns and flashes a reassuring smile. John Rogers is the point man for this raid on the labyrinth.

"Okay, pal, so here's the deal for Columbus. David Gregory from NBC is doing a segment for *The Today Show,* and he and his crew are gonna meet the car as we pull up. I know we said yes to a sit-down after the event, but he also wants to walk and talk you into the auditorium. As soon as you reach backstage, he'll fall back, and you'll have time to regroup."

Walk and talk? I'm not sure I can do a half-assed job of either, and doing both at once might trigger a synaptic meltdown. Droplets of sweat water-bomb a speech I pretend to study, but really just rattle between two clenched fists. *This pill isn't kicking in.* I appeal to the volunteer ex-cop, "Can we do a couple laps around the block, or the campus—or the state maybe?"

One five-minute circuit of OSU later, and it's evident that better living won't be achieved through chemistry anytime soon. I might as well get my shaky ass to the rally.

By dispatching David Gregory, NBC's chief White House correspondent, to Ohio to file this report, *The Today Show* adds their editorial weight to the increasing media affirmation that our push to elect pro–stem cell legislators is big-time political news, and not an entertainment story. The mainstream press is responsibly and evenhandedly moderating this unexpected national conversation. It is important, it is long overdue, and it is playing out not only on news broadcasts and political panel shows, but also in the home, the coffee shop, the office, down at the plant, and on the sidelines of kids' soccer games. Celebrity may have been what first attracted the cameras and reporters, but what is carrying us beyond sideshow curiosity, to use the political vernacular, is our ability to stay on message. Admittedly the context is complex and bears careful consideration, but from our point of view, the right to hope is simple.

. . .

David Gregory is a tall man—not even tall*ish,* just tall. I am a short man and likewise can claim no *ish,* but even without my brevity for contrast, David Gregory is needlessly tall. This perverts a "walk and talk"; to hold us both in frame for the *walk,* the cameraman has to stay ten steps ahead, trailing a perilous length of cable begging to be trampled or tangled around an ankle. As for the *talk,* I don't know how the boom operator can record us equally without the microphone bludgeoning Gregory at the hairline. There's an old Hollywood saying, "A short actor stands on a box, but a short movie star has everyone else stand in a ditch." There is no time to dig ditches, and besides, there's more to it than flawed composition. Factor in my Parkinsonian gait, and the whole inelegant procession is even less ready for prime time. The levodopa I've taken has yet to breach the blood-brain barrier, so I proceed in a stiff, straight-armed, lurching shuffle. It's as though a rope anchored beneath the crown of my head pulls me along at a speed not of my choosing. Sometimes, I appear to be warding off an incipient forward stumble without the good sense or basic reflexes to extend my arms for balance. Neurologists call this Parkinson's-related movement disorder "bradykinesia." Symptoms also make it difficult to raise my unblinking eyes or glance peripherally at my interrogator. With my face semi-frozen under the PD mask, responding audibly, articulately, or with much inflection at all is a challenge. Nothing to do with David Gregory—okay, would it kill the guy to slouch?—I just hate mixing shoe leather and interviews. As for mixing politics and Parkinson's—if I'm gonna mumble the mumble, I gotta stumble the stumble.

The next morning on *Today,* Gregory's voice-over will open: "Monday morning, Columbus, Ohio, week two in the political cross fire for Michael J. Fox." I don't know about "cross fire"—

from my vantage point all the shots seem to be from one direction, and anyway, "cross fire" implies that I got caught wandering clueless and uninvited into the middle of someone else's fight. Some on the other side of the stem cell debate, especially those who identify their position more for political convenience than out of a consistently demonstrated ethical concern, wish we would just go away. We are interlopers out of left field, hijacking airtime, page space, and fleeting public attention during the all-important denouement of the campaign.

Backstage at the law school, I'm introduced to Representative Sherrod Brown and his wife, Connie Schultz, the Pulitzer Prize–winning columnist. We've barely exchanged hellos when Gregory slips in with questions—a reminder that he didn't win his Emmy nomination loitering in corridors. Brown, unfazed by the intrusion into our face time, repeats what he has just told me: he will work hard in the Senate to help correct present government policy, not merely on human embryonic stem cell research, but in all fields of scientific study. For my part, I'm just happy to be *standing* and talking. A few more questions and it's time to get started. Staffers politely wrangle the candidate away; the room clears, and I'm led down to the auditorium stage.

The program is under way. Representative Brown and Ms. Schultz have taken seats alongside various dignitaries, doctors, researchers, patients, and advocates. Present too are a number of school-aged children and their parents. One of these kids, eleven-year-old Tanner Barton, is invited to speak at a podium he can barely peer over. With beguiling self-possession, Tanner describes the painful routine of a diabetic: the needles, the isolation from his peers, the hours in dialysis, and the stigma of different-ness.

Diabetes researchers are working with stem cells to develop an alternative source of pancreatic islets cells (insulin-producing cells). The goal is to transform embryonic stem cells into real live functional pancreatic cells and one day be able to transplant these cells into patients. Too much precious time and energy has gone into maneuvering around the road-blocks put in place by current procedural restrictions on this promising research.

Tanner isn't getting into the science, just what his life is like with JD and his hope to one day get better. I'm thinking that Tanner doesn't get to talk about this stuff often and never to a packed auditorium in front of microphones and TV cameras. He's making the most of his opportunity. As he lets it all out, it's obvious that he's a tough kid, but it's also easy to discern the uncertainty beneath his boyish bravado.

Now, I'm not kidding myself about the context in which this is all taking place. Sherrod Brown is the Democratic candidate for a currently Republican-held U.S. Senate seat in the battle-ground state of Ohio during the closing days of a midterm election. By no means are we on neutral ground; there is, admittedly, no "debate" here in Columbus today. I think it's a stretch, however, to view Tanner's message, or mine for that matter, in a strictly partisan or even political light. This is a sensitive issue, and the ethical concerns raised by the opponents of embryonic stem cell research are heartfelt and, personally speaking, deeply respected. I acknowledge the fact that my own views are subjective. I have a stake in this argument that some may fairly say disqualifies me from giving both sides of the argument equal weight. You yourself may have thoughtfully considered the issue and arrived at the conclusion that embryonic stem cell research is wrong and that, at the very least, it is not something you want the government to support. As frustrated as we in the patient community are with impediments to progress put in place by George W. Bush, so too are you frustrated that we, the proponents, just don't get it, that we're missing the bigger picture. In that way, we two can empathize with each other, while not agreeing. This is why I brought into the political arena my concerns and my hopes that this work can produce cures and treatments, not to shame or ridicule those who disagree with me, and not to use the bully pulpit of celebrity to drown out anyone else's voice. The opposite is true. What we want is a conversation. The only way for government to express the needs and desires of Americans is if Americans speak up and get involved. And as much as I want to make my own points, to express my own needs and desires, I know it's crucial that differing opinions be given equal hearing.

Polling indicates, however, that those in opposition represent the minority. And so, from a political perspective, it comes down to numbers, and by numbers, I mean, of course, votes. People often ask me, why then, if most Americans favor federally funded stem cell research, don't we have the numbers to prevail? Good question. What seems like basic arithmetic is actually a complicated exercise in electoral math. Each vote represents a multitude of beliefs, ethical concerns, complaints, fears, wants, and needs, in an order of personal importance unique to that voter. The calculus for a candidate and his or her strategists is to figure out which issues that citizen, as part of the larger matrix, is willing to abandon or put aside for another cycle, and conversely, which magic combination will inspire him or her to go to the polls and pull the desired lever. Figure that citizen A is liberal to moderate, favors stem cell research, and on his list of the big ten issues, puts it at eight. Citizen B, a religious Conservative, anti–stem cell research, is probably going to have it in his top three. In a close race, a canny, uncommitted pol, with no strong personal commitment to one side or the other, does the math and feigns fear of the prospect of cloning. This doesn't help either side.

But that is the subtle manipulation at play here. And so to counter it means taking our message and our own set of numbers into the political realm. We need a veto-proof margin in both houses to pass the Stem Cell Research Enhancement Act. There is nothing secretive about our aim: reach voters who have a positive association with science and research that could bring potential cures, and contrast that disposition with their local candidate's record. We also examine how the candidate's stance on stem cells fits the profile of his or her positions on related ethical concerns. Especially relevant is the question of whether the candidate opposes the destruction of embryos but supports in vitro fertilization. In vitro fertilization creates a surplus of embryos, which are *discarded* in numbers greater than will ever be used in research. Many of our friends are parents of beautiful children who, without in vitro, would not exist—I have no reservations about it. However, to favor one and forbid the other is fundamentally inconsistent, or plainly inequitable.

A head-to-head election matching a pro–stem cell candidate

against one who opposes stem cell research represents our best opportunity to remind people that we're not talking in the abstract. This issue affects them as well as one hundred million other Americans, for whom it rises to the level of life or death. One thing we absolutely are not saying is that those on the other side of the issue have any less compassion, empathy, or concern for those who are sick and suffering. I know that many who oppose embryonic stem cell research feel strongly that theirs is a truly compassionate position. Politicians, however, by exploiting medical research as a "wedge issue," hold the future hostage. That's why I came to Columbus this morning and will go to Iowa this afternoon, Maryland tomorrow, Virginia, Wisconsin, and Arizona throughout the week. Incurable disease is a nonpartisan problem that will require a bipartisan solution. The desire to alleviate suffering and save lives speaks not to our allegiance to any party or ideology but to our humanity.

The applause as young Tanner concludes his speech carries him all the way to his chair, where his dad pulls him close for a hug. A parent can't shield a child from pain or illness; only love him, as Tanner's father clearly does, and fight what fights he can on his behalf. The idea that this eleven-year-old boy, his father, or any of the patients and families here today are being manipulated or are manipulating anyone else is absurd. Not one word Tanner spoke today was spoon-fed or programmed. These words, however, just so there's no confusion, are mine: Tanner wants an end to the tyranny of juvenile diabetes within his lifetime. Right on, kid. *Sic semper tyrannus!*

In a narrow vestibule, really a small set of stairs at the perimeter of the stage, I'm awaiting my cue. Unfortunately *my* tyrant still has me under a boot heel. It may be the stress of travel and time in front of the press, but my "offs"—that is, the periods of time when the drugs aren't working—are lasting so long that I have to answer with a surfeit of medication. This induces rollicking dyskinesias. It's a balancing act, but given the Hobson's choice between the rocking, bobbing, and weaving of dyskinesias and the shaking, shuffling, and mumbling of bradykinesia, rocking is, believe it or not, the more comfortable option, if only by a razor-thin margin.

Clustered around me in the stairwell are assorted Brown campaign staffers and volunteers, members of the press, and my own humble retinue of advisors and aides-de-camp—John Rogers, of course, Tricia Brooks and Alan McCleod from his staff, and my assistant, Jackie Hamada. Last-minute instructions and random bits of information whispered into my ear quickly pass through to the other side and out into the ether. My performer's instincts kick in and my attention shifts to the crowd.

Spying around a partition wall earns an unobstructed view. A palpable energy percolates through the full house, evident in the undulating wave of placards: "LIFT RESTRICTIONS ON STEM CELLS," "WE WANT OUR CURES," "MAKE THE PRO-<u>LIVING</u> CHOICE," and for comic relief, I suppose, "MJF FOR PRESIDENT." I remain transfixed and slightly confused by what I see. And then it registers—something sets this group apart from those at other political rallies I have attended. So many attendees of every age and ethnicity are in wheelchairs, the youngest of them probably victims of spinal cord injury. Some labored to get here with walkers and canes. My fellow Parkinson's patients are present in number too. I have no trouble spotting them, not just by the tremors, but also by the same slightly forward-leaning, stooped-shouldered posture that I have surrendered to for the moment. Older folks stand next to caregivers and family members and gaze blankly ahead with the thousand-mile stare of Alzheimer's. I'm still trying to connect the scene to a larger tableau, a further "something familiar," and it takes a few more beats before it finally registers. *My God, it's a revival meeting.* The association, once made, sticks. I can't shake it. In my life, quite recently in fact, I've experienced revival meetings, and the only details missing here are shopping carts full of discarded crutches and a platoon of ushers with wireless transmitters, shepherding the afflicted into lines to be processed onto the stage. That's not happening here, of course. But in what way would that flock really be any different from this flock? Gathering at an Ohio University auditorium or in a Houston-based megachurch, haven't people the same desire for healing, a release from sickness, a cure? The answer lies somewhere between faith and hope, between seeking change through a petition of God and seeking it through an exercise of political franchise.

I hold two very different pieces of paper in hands that are, for the moment, not trembling. One is my speech, now a sweat-blotted Rorschach test, totally useless, unless the gist of my comments is "naked lady with a chain saw." At the other end of the pictorial spectrum is a piece of paper just handed to me by a little girl named Jessi. It's a watercolor painting, a series of portraits of Jessi's heroes: her teacher, her doctor, her parents, and a fairly passable likeness of me. She says it comes with a hug, and while I bend down to receive delivery, Jackie scoops up the artwork for safekeeping. It will soon be framed and displayed in my office. When I am at last called to the podium, the crowd erupts—clapping, shouting, whistling, and waving their signage. After a breath, I close my eyes for another second. *How on earth did I get here?*

Christopher Moved

In another lifetime, prior to our respective health disasters, Christopher Reeve and I were movie stars. And like all smart Hollywood people, we lived in New York. We'd see each other around at events, premieres, and an occasional party. In the spring of 1993, Tracy and I shared a booth with Chris and Dana at the opening of a Planet Hollywood restaurant in London. Just married, they were a smart, funny, gracious, and ridiculously good-looking couple. Tracy mentioned to me later how sweet and unabashedly smitten with each other they were, and I agreed, registering the subtle hint to be more demonstrative in affections toward my own bride. Two years later, when Chris was paralyzed in a fall from his horse during an equestrian event, we felt anguish and profound disbelief. How could this happen to Chris, an expert horseman, doing what he loved to do, just as he had done thousands of times before? That such a mensch, a good and decent man, a father, a husband, could be touched by this random life-changing calamity seemed to validate the dread we feel when a spouse is late driving home on a rainy night, or a kid takes too long to scramble up from a spill on the playground.

For weeks after Chris was hurt, it seemed that the press and public alike would never tire of strained allusions to his *Superman* persona and the "bitter irony" of it all. But while so many were preoccupied with the "superhero suffers real human tragedy" angle, few anticipated the actual flesh-and-blood hero Christopher Reeve would become. Chris defined hero as "an ordinary individual who finds the strength to persevere and endure." In spite of Chris's humility, some idealized his heroism as preordained and could not be dissuaded by the "ordinary individual" argument. Well-meaning people, struggling to make sense of the senseless, assured Chris that the accident had happened to him for a reason, which only added another burden to his physical, emotional, and financial load—the weight of anointing.

Michael Manganiello, a tireless stem cell advocate, who had covered this territory for years as one of Chris and Dana's closest advisors, remembers the couple refuting the attribution of Chris's quadriplegia to a higher purpose. "No, this just sucks. It doesn't happen to anybody for a reason. Sometimes bad things happen, but it's how you deal with those things that matters." Though never shy about speaking his mind, even with the imperfect assistance of his respirator, Chris knew his most powerful statement would be wordless. "Chris wanted to get out of his chair, and Dana wanted Chris to get out of his chair," Mike says. Dedication to that eventuality came second only to their dedication to each other and their family. "Chris became a symbol for people with spinal cord injury and other disabilities, and Dana became a symbol to caregivers around the world. Life can still be good. It's all about how you face the challenges." Chris and Dana gave us all a tutorial on courage, resilience, love, and always hope.

People are sometimes surprised to learn that we didn't know each other all that well. There were some phone calls in the years between my PD disclosure and Chris's passing, maybe a half dozen or more, most of them business-related. We never really opened it up beyond that. When the person on the other end of the line can't breathe without mechanical assistance, I'm not expecting casual banter. We did talk hockey, though—my beloved ancestral sport. His son Will played, while my son, Sam, never took it up. I'd get a vicarious kick out of Chris, who never missed a game, doing the proud hockey-dad bit. The common objectives of our two research foundations provided the usual pretext. With more to learn from Chris than he'd ever learn from me, I'd tend to be circumspect as he outlined how to influence policy or rated the reliability of this senator or that congresswoman. I remember how I fixated on not interrupting him, though I inevitably would anyway. Chris was so articulate and careful in choosing his words, meticulously stringing together garlands of thought with a rhythm and timing I just assumed to be his own. Then he'd pause, and I'd respond in the gap, only to hear the wheezing *hiss-pop* of his respirator recycling and then Chris's quiet, halting voice, picking up where he left off. This played out once or twice every call. I'd be embarrassed, but if it bothered him at all, he was too polite to say (or maybe he did and I cut him off). Eventually I learned to internalize the timing of the oxygen being forced in and out of Chris's larynx. It kept him alive, but he wasn't breathing—

actively taking in air. Entrusted with life-and-death responsibility, ungoverned by an operating conscience, with all the emotional investment of a digital clock, the respirator gave Chris the breath to live. But Chris's end of the transaction was anything but mechanical. He gave life to the breath—oxygen, a simple gas, he transformed into words, ideas, hope. The last one and the next weren't important, *this one was*. From each fresh serving, Chris drew the patience and spirit to look past the everyday tasks he could no longer do and envision himself accomplishing what had never been done.

A paradox reoccurred with each call—I'd be in my office, a one-man riot of motion, trying to wrest control of my extremities from the grip of PD, while Chris, in his home, sat forcibly quiescent. Truth is, Chris's stillness scared the shit out of me. Parkinson's, no matter how hellish the dance, inexorably takes you to stillness. Whenever I had the privilege of sharing time and place with Chris, I looked for a moment to talk with him about the stillness, how lonely it must be. I never found that moment. A scheduled co-appearance before Congress in the fall of 2000 held out promise that we'd have more time than in the past, but an illness forced him to cancel the trip to DC. In his absence, I was asked to read into the Congressional Record Chris's statement advocating fewer restrictions on scientific research.

One way to appreciate the difference between what happened to Chris and what was uncoiling in my life would be to analogize the sudden impact of a locomotive with the incremental awareness of being tied to the tracks, and feeling the vibration from the approaching train, with no way to gauge its proximity. Because Chris's injury had been sustained instantaneously, he could only react to what he could not undo, whereas I had time to anticipate what I could not avoid.

Externals and vagaries of timing aside, Chris focused not on the "What happened?" but on the "What now?" "Before a catastrophe, we can't imagine coping with the burdens that might confront us in a dire moment. Then when that moment arrives, we suddenly find that we have resources inside us that we knew nothing about," he said. There was nothing sudden about it, but with growing assuredness, I began to plumb those resources. The important thing, I realized, was to avoid panic, and I couldn't find a more powerful example of sublime grace under unrelenting pressure than Christopher Reeve.

The 2004 Bush v. Kerry presidential election was the last one Chris Reeve would ever see, and sadly he didn't see it through to its completion (not that he would have been happy with the result). On October 10, 2004, thirty-four days before the election, Chris succumbed to cardiac arrest. A few days later, I sat next to Teresa Heinz Kerry in Arizona as we watched her husband in a debate with George Bush. When the press asked me afterward to comment on Chris's passing and its effect on stem cell advocacy, I found myself overcome with emotion and, after mumbling a perfunctory answer, excused myself. Chris spent the better—and the worst—part of his life exemplifying the power of advocacy in a democracy, proving by example that if one speaks up on issues they care about, they will motivate others to do the same. I heard that Chris had been under some pressure not to get involved in the 2004 election. When I asked Mike Manganiello about this, he told me, "Chris worried that patients and researchers might suffer if he got involved in the election. The Christopher Reeve Foundation received a great deal of federal money, plus there was legislation with Chris's name on it, and if Chris got partisan, all of it was at risk. In the end, he just felt he couldn't. When he died that October, Dana said, 'I have to go campaign for Kerry.' So, we took her to Ohio, and she gave a speech that is indelibly imprinted on me. It was one of those moments. Chris always said, 'I'm one guy, I'm a voice for those people, but they're all out there to carry on the message.'"

Though no one could have known or believed it then, it would be Dana's last campaign as well. Though a nonsmoker, she was diagnosed with lung cancer in the summer of 2005. In pushing back against those constraints that Chris had struggled with, she gave a heartfelt gift to her late husband and to everyone for whom stem cell research may hold the key to a longer, healthier life. Chris's passing was hard, Dana's too, so sudden and unfair. But they inspired us all to move forward.

Who Do You Trust?

With few exceptions, everybody likes to be liked. This is especially true for actors. Even those whom we don't think of as likeable, whose on-screen or off-screen personas seem dark or inaccessible, at the very least have the quality of their work to recommend them—"He's a jerk, but I liked him in that movie."

When Sally Field burbled, "You like me . . . right now, you like me," in acceptance of her 1984 Best Actress Oscar for *Places in the Heart,* her earnest expression of surprise at the Academy's approbation inspired press reactions ranging from good-natured kidding to accusations of typical Hollywood narcissism. The public, for the most part, agreed with Sally—except maybe for the "right now" qualification; they liked her before, they've liked her since, and they still like her now. They may have been a little confused that a popular actress at the pinnacle of her career would still have doubts. Actors in the audience though—myself included—understood the manifest relief in her realization that all of her sacrifice, effort, and perseverance had paid off in a treasure far greater than a golden statuette or more offers coming in to her agent—it was a pat on the back.

Audiences had come to trust that Sally Field would deliver compelling, nuanced performances when the cameras were rolling and not be a complete pain in the ass when they weren't. This is directly connected to the same trust that they have in the now gracefully maturing Sally Field when she pitches Boniva for warding off osteoporosis. For the advertising industry, always on the hunt for effective spokesmen and -women, the key to the successful pairing of a celebrity spokesperson with his or her target consumer is the quality of that trust—as well as the quantity. Yes, trust is now quantifiable.

Since the early days of television and radio, companies such as Nielsen or Arbitron have measured the size and demographic breakdown of audiences. Something called a "Q-rating" combines the name recognition of a particular celebrity or public figure with the emotional reaction elicited by that name—favorable or unfavorable—to establish a ranking. Recently though, market researchers have taken this metric to a new level with the specific goal of determining not just how much we like a particular celebrity, but, more importantly for advertisers, also how much we trust them.

Of course, the accuracy and relevance of this data is debatable, but the full list, called "The Davie Brown Index (DBI)," can be accessed by advertisers for twenty thousand a year. In terms of marketing budgets, that's just a drop in the bucket. Whether it was leaked or planted, the DBI was picked up and reported on by several media outlets, and in February of 2006, *New York* magazine published a portion of its findings. A friend faxed me a copy of the article after having circled the name at number four on the list after Tom Hanks, Oprah, and Bill Cosby and just ahead of Michael Jordan—it was me.

Now I'm not gonna lie (*trust me*)—this was a nice and unexpected affirmation, certainly better than landing in the top five "All-time Assholes List." For over two decades, I've benefited in almost every conceivable fashion from the overwhelming goodwill of millions of people I've never met. Over the course of a long career, sometimes the box office has been good, and sometimes it hasn't; sometimes I've been at the top of the ratings, and sometimes in the cellar. But since the first season of *Family Ties,* people have, as Sally put it, "liked me." I had never considered the jump from "liking" to "trusting" or even "respecting." Beyond a hello, a handshake, and a "loved *Teen Wolf,*" anything else folks thought of me was none of my business. But, as evidenced by the DBI and the appetite among advertisers for this information, for some, it *is* business. Any savvy executive will tell you that business and politics don't mix.

Look at that list again. Tom Hanks, a genuinely nice guy,

is known for his everyman and often patriotic roles—no controversy there. Oprah studiously avoided involvement in the world of politics until her recent endorsement of Barack Obama (I suspect that caused her to drop a few spots). Bill Cosby, to many Americans, personifies the comforts and strengths of the nuclear family. Michael Jordan, when pressed to explain his staunch avoidance of any political actions or statements, said simply, "Republicans buy sneakers, too." As for me, I suppose the DBI should have been my cue to leverage some of this trust on behalf of some toothpaste company or noodle manufacturer, but I didn't do that. I just had a laugh and slipped the list into my shred pile.

Six months later, though, I put that trust to the test and my "likability" at risk by, in effect, becoming a pitchman for scientific freedom and stem cell research. Many people who had been in my corner for years remained there and became more vocal in their support, but there was definitely a significant contingent that "fell out of like" with me. I have made no effort to measure the fallout, and no, I haven't looked at last year's list—got an extra twenty thousand bucks? After all, the substance of why people had a rapport with me or a feeling of trust was nothing that I cultivated or would have thought to manufacture if it were not organic. It was the happy residue of me being true to myself.

Even with the ubiquity that comes from showing up on endless television reruns and rented DVDs, I now think of myself as more of a father, husband, patient, activist, and citizen than as a celebrity. And to my great delight and satisfaction, the early successes and strong reputation of the Michael J. Fox Foundation had more to do with the talents and dedication of our staff than the famous name on the door.

In a strange way, I think of my political activities on behalf of stem cell research as more personal than public. I saw a need and sought to address it in the most effective way I could, by whatever legitimate means necessary. The stakes were too high to worry about whether ten, a hundred, a thousand, or even a million people would like me less if I got involved. Not that I was so brave that I could have taken this on without an example to follow.

When both Chris and Dana were gone, I felt it was no small responsibility but a great privilege to carry on their work as best I could. There is a quote from Chris that stayed with me long after his passing: "Either you decide to stay in the shallow end of the pool, or you go out in the ocean." I tried toe-dipping, wading, treading, a few tentative strokes, and then, as if unconsciously following Chris's advice, I found myself in some very deep, very rough water. Funny, Chris didn't mention the sharks.

Vineyard 2001: A Shot Across the Bow

MARTHA'S VINEYARD, MASSACHUSETTS

SUMMER 2001

My son, Sam, then ten years old, had just rejoined us on Martha's Vineyard from sleepaway camp. He was the battery's powder man, confidently tamping a generous load of the potassium nitrate, sulfur, and carbon mixture into the touch hole of the cannon, which pointed in an indiscriminate backyardly direction from the high ground of our porch. Hunkering down to light the fuse, pyro expert and erstwhile Clinton Communications Director George Stephanopoulos struck a kitchen match with his thumbnail and brought the bud of its flame to meet the wick. (Okay, I made up the thumbnail part.) Sam and George grinned grins I can only characterize as disquieting.

Retreat seemed prudent—an offer to get cold drinks would provide cover—but out of some vague sense of fatherly duty, I said, "Careful, guys, it's all fun and games till somebody blows a hand off."

Before I could follow up with the always hilarious "and then it's just fun," a shockingly loud roar leapt from the throat of the cannon, echoing off the dunes before rolling down to the shore. A thin wisp of black smoke trailed after, but the breeze soon took it. A quick check for missing hands was preempted by the sound of all four applauding the success of their owners. The truth is, it was a little replica cannon, a weapon of minimal destruction. There wasn't even a projectile involved. At worst, a misfire might cost a finger.

Now, if you're a father reading this, you're probably asking, "Why didn't Mike help Sam fire the cannon?" (Too shaky.) *If you're a kid and you're reading this, which is okay, I guess, you're probably asking, "Where do I get a cannon?"* (From a pirate.) *If you're a mother, you're probably screaming, "You let them play with a freaking cannon?!"* (. . . What cannon?) *But if you're a political junkie, like me, you're saying, "Wait . . . George Stephanopoulos?"* (I'll get to that part in a minute.)

"Dad," Sam asked, using the instep of his Nike to sweep the excess gunpowder between the porch's floorboards, instantly designating this the nonsmoking area, "if we did blow our hands off, could stem cells grow them back?"

With a quick glance toward me, George smiled. He wanted to hear the answer to this one too.

On this July weekend, George Stephanopoulos had come to Martha's Vineyard to interview me for the Sunday morning political program *This Week with Sam Donaldson and Cokie Roberts.* ABC hadn't yet replaced those two legendary names with "Stephanopoulos," so George was still pulling field duty. Tracy and I had known George since before I served as his doppelganger in *The American President,* and we talked him out of staying at a hotel to be our houseguest for the evening. We had conducted the interview earlier in the day, and the locale beat any TV studio, with an azure sky and the post-card Edgartown Marina as the backdrop. George had come to discuss stem cells, which made for an odd pairing of setting and subject matter. The future of the research hinged on President Bush's impending policy decision. With the policy profile of the new administration still somewhat inchoate and enigmatic, George's inquiry centered on expectation and guess-work. The President might unveil restrictions or a surprising show of support, but an outright ban was also possible. It's hard to remember when war, reasons for war, and rumors of new wars didn't dominate headlines. But in that last pre-9/11 summer of 2001, as George puts it, "Gary Condit, sharks, and stem cells" were the media's obsessions.

For two years prior to the policy announcement in 2001, attention was focused on stem cells, not by the general public or the media, perhaps, but by those who in one way or another had a stake in the science. Experts were empaneled, congressional hearings convened, fact-finding committees found fact, each endeavoring to unravel the promise from the controversy and reconcile the theory with practical application. Over all of it hung an air of deliberate delay. It was an emerging science, and much of the lab work wouldn't be a practical reality until the beginning of the twenty-first century, so while Clinton favored embryonic stem cell research, everyone seemed to be waiting out Clinton's term to find out where the "new guy" stood. Those of us living with and dying from diseases and conditions presently incurable are aware that our situation is not time-neutral. One activist Parkinson's patient, Jim Kordy, is well known on Capitol Hill for carrying an oversized hourglass into meetings and committee chambers, flipping it over and, as the sands run out, demanding that attention be paid to Parkinson's disease and the evanescent nature of time.

I addressed this perceived congressional foot-dragging in September of 2000 when, along with Mary Tyler Moore, the late Jennifer Estess of Project ALS (actress Gina Gershon read Jennifer's statement aloud for her), and others, I testified before a Senate labor, health, and education appropriations subcommittee. After first reading Chris Reeve's remarks into the record, I used the privilege of my allotted time to vent a modicum of spleen. "For two years, you have had a parade of witnesses—scientists, ethicists, theologians of every school, and some celebrities discussing every nuance of stem cell research. You've given time to all sides of the issue, including the few but very vocal opponents. But the consistent and inescapable conclusion is that this research offers the potential to eliminate diseases—literally save millions of lives. So, while I applaud your thoroughness, I can't help but say, respectfully: 'Enough!' "

Less than a week before the 2000 election, the *New York Times* published an editorial I had written, limning the frustration and promise associated with stem cell research. I reminded the then governor of Texas, George W. Bush, and the voting public that should he win, he'd have the opportunity to introduce historic policy on stem cells. Throughout the campaign his advisors had counseled him not to touch the issue, viewing it as a third rail. We patient advocates urged him to eschew political ass-covering and declare his position. I was more politic in my message to the soon-to-be President-elect, which read, in part:

A Crucial Election for Medical Research—
New York Times—*November 1, 2000*

Mr. Bush favors a ban on stem cell research, one aide said, "because of his pro-life views."

Yet stem cell research has nothing to do with abortion . . . [It] uses undifferentiated cells extracted from embryos just a few days old—embryos produced during in vitro fertilization . . . Currently, more than 100,000 embryos are frozen in storage. Most of these microscopic clumps of cells are destined to be destroyed—ending any potential for life . . .

Support for stem-cell research comes not just from pro-choice Democrats like Al Gore but also from Republicans who have concluded, in the words of former Senator Bob Dole, that supporting such research is "the pro-life position to take."

. . . One hopes that between now and next Tuesday, Mr. Bush will explain to those of us with debilitating diseases—indeed, to all of us—why it is more pro-life to throw away stem cells than to put them to work saving lives.

Candidate Bush soon became President Bush. While George Stephanopoulos and I were conducting our Q & A on Martha's Vineyard, the new President and his counsel were shaping the administration's stem cell policy. We were looking for signs and, finding none, were still hopeful.

THE BUSH RANCH / WESTERN WHITE HOUSE, CRAWFORD, TEXAS · AUGUST 9, 2001

Speaking from Crawford, Texas, the President, in the first major policy announcement of his administration, addressed what he called a "complex and difficult issue . . . one of the most profound of our time": embryonic stem cell research. In many ways, it was an excellent speech, delivered in language crafted to mollify both camps. He made references to "the Creator," "moral hazards," and "ethical ramifications," adding, "I have made this decision with great care and I pray it is the right one." The spiritual tone sent a message to his Christian conservative base that he hadn't abandoned them.

Pro–stem cell Americans, millions battling incurable illness (including, I'm sure, some Evangelicals and conservative Catholics whose prayers have led them to embrace the promise of embryonic stem cell research), heard a welcome message too:

the President would allow the research to continue. While certainly good news on its surface, key elements of the new policy were troubling and raised yellow flags, if not red ones quite yet. Qualifications limited all researchers to only the currently existing self-replicating colonies of stem cells, known as "cell lines." The NIH had informed the President the latest estimate was approximately sixty cell lines, but our research had the actual number that were viable much lower: fewer than twenty, perhaps as few as thirteen. No federally funded research was to be done to discover newer lines, nor was any research with new lines, even if it received no federal money, allowed in any facility or institution that received a single tax dollar for any purpose. That's a big "nor." It meant that if a stem cell scientist still hadn't been discouraged enough to quit the work, but wanted to maintain ties to a funded institution, he or she had to duplicate staff and facilities off-premises. Another vital concern with these existing cell lines was their purity. Some, if not most, were sure to be contaminated by non-human proteins. These proteins, often from mouse cells, made certain lines useless for developing therapies that could be translated to human patients.

Inherent in what the President was describing were still other trapdoors on the paths to cures. One of these trapdoors would be dealing with private ownership of the cell lines. We knew this would compromise timely progress, as private labs and corporations are reticent about sharing with outside researchers. In a telephone conversation with health and human services secretary Tommy Thompson, the day after the speech, I said we were glad the President acknowledged the promise of stem cell research, but had serious unanswered questions. The secretary, whom we knew to be a proponent of embryonic stem cell research (since then, he pursued the Republican presidential nomination and adopted a more conservative–friendly position . . . *Tommy doin' the calculus*), said that the NIH reported to him personally that there were, in fact, sixty-nine lines available worldwide. The NIH seems to have provided a different number than the one they had given the President. As to proprietary rights, he assured us that while there was not yet a formal agreement, the private and corporate groups were *expected* to cooperate. Secretary Thompson admitted that there remained some questions about fees and payment for privately owned cell lines. The net effect of the President's cell-line provisos would be, we feared, a limit in the quantity and quality of available cells, and diminished expectations.

I was disappointed, but I still thought, *Better than nothing, let's wait and see.*

Maybe the policy was so clever in its design, so deft a head-fake by George W. Bush, that the plan was to make us think both sides had given a little, when all along, science was intended to take the loss.

For the next four years, not many people were especially concerned with stem cells, except for those of us whose lives may depend on them. The issue did surface during the '04 presidential election. I did an ad for Kerry, which attracted little attention. Perhaps it was because I also cut an ad for a Republican senator, Arlen Specter, or more likely because voters were focusing on Al Qaeda sleeper cells and not embryonic stem cells. Dana Reeve gave her brave and defiant speech in

Ohio on her late husband's behalf. There was a significant victory in California: Proposition 71, an initiative to establish the California Institute for Regenerative Medicine, passed by 59 percent, committing a three-billion-dollar bond issue to support embryonic stem cell research in the state. Nationally, legislation was introduced in Congress to reform the stem cell policy, add new cell lines, and increase present federal funding, without success.

All the while, the restrictions from 2001, acting like a poison pill, brought research to a virtual standstill. Private foundations did what they could. The Michael J. Fox Foundation took the lead in promoting stem cell research as it related to Parkinson's disease. We funded a four-million-dollar initiative to advance research using all stem cell types. Our goal was to determine which, of any, of these cell types had the greatest potential for Parkinson's. Results were clear; in several experiments embryonic stem cells showed the most promise, as they were much more easily manipulated into the dopamine-producing neurons needed to repair the brain.

Even with our own advances, the freeze imposed by Bush's restrictive policy meant that critical next experiments could not take place. The next hurdle would have needed far greater support than an individual foundation could provide.

.   .   .

Our little, shingled Martha's Vineyard saltbox is blessed with an unobstructed view of the Gay Head Lighthouse. Every night its beacon slowly turns, and each half revolution paints the house and hillside with a warm swath of light. From dusk onward, fireflies twinkle through the grasses like Bush forty-one's metaphorical "Thousand Points of Light." The beacon completes another thirty-second sweep of the nightscape, and a wave of brilliance washes out the glow of the insects. A thousand fireflies won't generate the luminescence sufficient to read a roadmap. A lighthouse—more powerful and dependable—speaks to the guiding nature of hope. By equal turns, it illuminates and darkens, so the way forward can be chosen in the light, and trusted in the darkness.

Admittedly, I haven't spent much time in West Texas, but given the amount and variety of brush the President clears on his vacations, my guess is that he has a lot of fireflies on that ranch—*and no lighthouse.*

Vineyard 2006: Groundhog Day

MARTHA'S VINEYARD · SUMMER 2006

I tossed the cooler bag, filled with empties—sandwich wrappers, a medley of Tupperware containers, water bottles, and soda cans—onto the kitchen island and took two quick shuffle steps to the pie safe upon which our kitchen telephone resides. I hit the playback button on the answering machine. Its cheerful inner-robot informed me that I had five new messages. A quick glance over my sunburned shoulder elicited a wince, not out of pain but recognition of my flagrant breach of beach house etiquette. From the backdoor to where I now stood, my path was vividly described in wet sandy footprints.

—Beep. "This is Senator Reid's office calling for Michael J. Fox. Please call back at your convenience."

Tracy was still outside on the back porch, probably rinsing the sand off my youngest daughter Esmé's tiny feet.

—Beep. "Hey Pal, John Rogers here. Senator Reid's office is gonna call, you know what it's about."

. . . Tracy was probably going to ask if she has to rinse the sand off my tiny feet.

—Beep. "Hello, Senator Reid's office again, please let us know the best time to reach you."

—Beep. "Mike, this is Tom Harkin, we've got the vote coming up and . . . well, I think Harry Reid's gonna call you."

One message left . . .

—Beep. "Tracy, it's Jennifer, don't worry about the salmon. Clark will pick it up from Larsen's. We'll do that cilantro thing."

. . . Excellent!

Eager to destroy all evidence of my transgression, I reached over to the kitchen island and snagged a dishrag from the towel bar, dropped it on the closest sandy print, planted a foot, and started mopping. Then the phone rang. I could have let it go, but that would have brought Tracy rushing in to answer.

I snatched up the receiver. "Hello?"

"Hello, Michael Fox? I have Senator Reid for you."

I heard the rattle and squeak of the screen door opening. It was Tracy. "Oh, Mike, look at the floor."

Phone in hand, I turned sheepishly toward the window. "Uh, can you please ask the senator to hold for a second?—I have to rinse my feet."

John Rogers was right, I knew why Senator Reid was calling, and Senator Harkin, and my friends at CAMR (the Coalition for the Advancement of Medical Research) and PAN. The Stem Cell Research Enhancement Act, also known as H.R. 810, a bipartisan bill introduced into Congress in February of 2005 by Representatives Mike Castle (R-DE) and Diana Degette (D-CO), passed the House, 238–194, in May of 2006. The Senate was set to vote on their version in the next few days. While I had yet to speak with Senator Reid directly, the other calls were requests that I do a media press in support of the bill, and I expected his to follow suit. I had no qualms with H.R. 810; it was an excellent piece of legislation, precisely what we needed. The bottom line was, the bill would pass easily, but we needed a two-thirds margin, and even with an encouraging number of Republican votes, we wouldn't cross that threshold. And then, sure as a Vineyard gull will shit on a shiny new car, the President would veto.

I was overcome with the weary feeling of déjà vu. It was on the Vineyard in 2001 that George Stephanopoulos and I discussed emerging stem cell policy. Now I was in the same place, five years later, talking stem cells again, with a United States senator. When the President unveiled his guidelines in 2001, I was away from Martha's Vineyard for a few days of work in Los Angeles, just as I would be in 2006 on the day the bill would likely pass and the President would let us down again.

I wasn't exactly searching for more responsibilities to fill my time. Although I didn't manage its day-to-day operations, I was heavily involved in the broad work of the Michael J. Fox Foundation, which by this point had grown into the second largest funder of PD research in the world, after the federal government. We were relentless in pursuing a wide portfolio of potential breakthroughs, including but by no means exclusive to those involving stem cells.

I wanted to bury my head in the sand for six more weeks of summer, but first I had to splash a little sand from between my toes, and take a call from a senator.

"Michael," Senator Reid began, "we don't know each other well, but we need your help on this one." Flattered that he thought so much of me, I was still hesitant. He then outlined the situation with H.R. 810, the expected vote total, and the almost 100 percent chance that the President would veto. "We need to get you out there," he said. "People expect to hear from you. If you could do a press conference," he said, "and a few interviews, the morning shows, that sort of thing. That would be great."

For the second time in ten minutes, I winced.

"Well you think about it. I just want to tell you, you'd be doing us a big favor."

Ooh, he used the f-word. To a politician, favors are mother's milk. I thanked him for the call and told him I'd consider it and call him back soon.

I still believed that as a stand-alone issue, most Americans favored a revamp of the administration's stem cell policy. I based that partly on the warm or at least open-minded reception that I generally received as an advocate of that approach. But experience had taught me that the United States presidency is indeed, as advertised, the world's greatest seat of power. And if George Bush was determined to thwart H.R. 810, I had begun to accept that there was not much anyone could do about it. The president had clearly closed his mind on the subject, and the public, while agreeing with me in principle, had no practical option to mandate a change in policy. While my participation in the debate might have brought attention, it wouldn't bring any real leverage. It seemed to me that all we could do was wait out the remaining years of his second term and hope for more enlightened leadership the next time around. That 2006 was a midterm election year and that coming November would bring opportunity for change in the House and Senate hadn't occurred to me . . . yet.

I tried several times to follow up with Senator Reid, but didn't connect. Little did I know that, as a result of the midterm elections, the next time I talked to Senate Minority Leader Reid, he would be Senate *Majority* Leader Reid.

MANHATTAN BEACH, CALIFORNIA

JULY 19, 2006

If the prospect of spending part of my summer battling with the Bush administration evoked a response of "been there, done that," my return to a different arena seemed exotic and finite in an appealing way. Since my retirement from *Spin City*, I had taken a few acting gigs, including a guest appearance on the Charlie Sheen version of the show. Then in 2004, Bill Lawrence, co-creator as well as one of my producing partners on *Spin City* (with Gary Goldberg), had asked me to do a two-episode "arc" on his surreally funny *Scrubs* sitcom for NBC, and I had accepted. Playing a brilliant surgeon challenged by severe obsessive-compulsive disorder, I was able to affect symptoms for the character that somewhat masked my own. The experience wasn't a cakewalk by any means, and while my work on *Scrubs* reminded me of all that I loved about acting, so too did it remind me of why I set it aside. Filming was delayed on one or two occasions, if only for a few minutes, by symptoms that wouldn't respond to medication in a timely fashion. Some acting choices, emotional and physical, were undercut by the stubborn refusal of my brain and body to cooperate. There were not quite as many arrows in the quiver, but still enough to hit the target most of the time; under the right circumstances, I found I could piece together a decent performance.

A year or so later, when David Kelley, the producer of *Boston Legal,* called to see if I'd be interested in doing a three-episode arc, I read the script and signed on. I did the first episodes in October of 2005, and after they aired and were well received, I committed to doing a couple more the following summer. My plan was to be in L.A. for a week or so in July '06 for filming, at the same time that the President was expected to veto the Stem Cell Enhancement Act. This created for me a classic conflict of old and new identities—an acting career I hadn't fully let go of and an advocacy role that I hadn't fully embraced.

Busy at work on the set of *Boston Legal* when CNN ran the live feed of the veto ceremony, I thought I'd catch the coverage in the makeup trailer between scenes. "Hair and Makeup," the communal hub of any film or series production, is the first place you hit in the morning and the last stop at wrap, with a few drop-bys in between. Gossip is swapped over brutal coffee; gripes find sympathetic ears; actors without scenes together hang out and BS, and the TV's always on. Bill Shatner, Candice

Bergen, Julie Bowen, among others, sat and swiveled in the trailer's barber-style chairs, hard at work being groomed. I filled an empty seat and, after soliciting objections and hearing none, clicked the TV channel over to the local ABC affiliate. The story led the first segment out of a commercial break.

The opening image revealed the President, a middle-aged man-island amid a sea of small children, Gulliver in Lilliput. A dozen or more kids—infants and teething babies to three-year-old toddlers, some bigger ones too—scampered around and crawled on, over, and under the POTUS. They hung off his coat sleeves, tugged on his tie, and one or two fussed and cried in the arms of a parent. These adorable young citizens were the guests of honor at a White House East Room reception prior to the veto ceremony. "Snowflake Babies" is the collective name given to children born from frozen embryos that in vitro parents have offered for adoption. Every year, tens of thousands are left over from the in vitro process. Remember, while the word "embryo" seems to suggest something far more developed, these are ten-day-old clusters of two, four, or eight cells we're talking about here. They are created outside of a womb, and those cells not implanted are cryogenically stored and eventually discarded. For the couple or individual unable to produce children, adopting an embryo from this surplus is inarguably a terrific outcome. Logic suggests and research substantiates, however, that even at record rates, such adoptions would account for only a fraction of embryos produced, leaving thousands of cells with the potential to save billions of lives. Happy kids make good TV, but presenting adoption as an answer to the routine disposal of unwanted in vitro embryos is manipulation. The intended take-away being *If you're in favor of embryonic stem cell research, you're against Snowflake Babies.*

Commonly overshadowed by the dispute over embryonic stem cells is the near-consensus on the fundamentals. We agree on the ethical guidelines; we are against egg farming, against human reproductive cloning, and emphatically *for* Snowflake Babies. Our sole disagreement hinges on our opposition to destroying frozen embryos that could be used in research to save lives.

Research using cells derived from other less controversial sources, like umbilical cord and adult stem cells, shows great promise, but these sources have yet to show the versatility of embryonic stem cells. One of the most exciting recent strategies involves using skin cells that have been altered to become embryonic stem cells (or at least look like them). If successful, these new stem cell approaches could provide an unlimited source of genetically matched cells with the ability to generate all kinds of replacement tissues, but without a lot of the controversy around use of human embryonic stem cells. However, we do not know whether these other strategies will truly replace embryonic stem cells, and for the time being, we need to keep all options on the table and support work on many types of cells.

Cut to the President delivering his formal remarks: "I hold to the principle that we can harness the promise of technology without becoming slaves to technology and ensure that science serves the cause of humanity. If we are to find the right ways to advance ethical medical research, we must also be willing, when necessary, to reject the wrong ways." In fairness, this would be the place to cut to footage of mist-shrouded canisters of frozen embryos being opened, and their contents wasted. The President concludes—"For that reason, I must veto this bill." Now the money shot: the President wielding the veto pen. In striking down H.R. 810, the Stem Cell Research Enhancement Act, George Walker Bush exercised what was the first veto of his eventful administration.

At one end of the long rectangular box of mirrors, I sat so close to the ceiling-mounted Sony that I could see only reflected fragments of the others watching with me, but they made themselves heard. The President's closing comments elicited a smattering of boos and hisses. As a guest actor on a couple of episodes, I'd made new friends here who knew what this meant to me. (The question was, did I?) A makeup sponge, wet with foundation, arced over my head and dinged off the TV screen, besmudging the presidential forehead. As if to forestall a barrage, the image reverted to *les tres mignon Enfants de Neige*.

Back to the anchorman: "In a statement recorded prior to the President's veto, actor and activist Michael J. Fox had this to say about stem cell research and the likelihood that President Bush would veto the bill":

I find it frustrating that the President would use his first veto to thwart this research. It just seems a shame. I respect those who oppose this research, but they do represent a minority, and I think that to make a choice to protect millions of cells that are going to be destroyed anyway over protecting millions of living and

soon-to-be living citizens of this country—it's hard to
get around that.

Scaled-down though my media blitz may have been, it
reached the one person who needed to wake up and smell
the veto—me. The restlessness I felt, eyes set in a squint,
face flushed, and mouth wrapped into a sour curl, were
symptoms—but not of Parkinson's. Flatly, I was pissed off.
There was a quality to this latest setback, an almost blithe
detachment in the President's tone and demeanor. And the
parade of Snowflake Babies was a patent misdirection, a
false choice—as if a healthy Tanner Barton and an adopted
embryo were mutually exclusive.

> People really want this, they've considered it, they've
> prayed on it and they've thought about it, and I think
> you have to trust the American people, our scientists,
> our institutions, our facilities, to really do the right
> thing to lead the way with this.

The East Room of the White House is too small a venue to
hold the hundred million people whose fates were actually attached to that signing. Short of an invitation, they at least merit
acknowledgment. For Alzheimer's, Parkinson's, Huntington's,
ALS, multiple sclerosis, and juvenile diabetes sufferers, the ink
on that veto represents life's blood. For others not there, the
veto prolongs uncertainty. Somewhere in the country, a single
mom lives every day with the fear that she, her little girl, and
her mother with early-onset Alzheimer's are locked into a cycle
of genetic predisposition that may never be broken. The

seventeen-year-old lifeguard who dove into the Long Island surf and broke his neck on a sandbar wasn't there to witness his hope to someday walk or surf again being consigned to the presidential outbox. These realities are tougher to look at than Snowflake Babies, but they are far more relevant.

We need leadership from the top to spur us on.

George W. Bush has always maintained that his decisions are informed by faith, and guided by ethical concern. His moral compass directed him in 2001 to boldly cite the promise of embryonic stem cell research and permit it, then to hinder progress in the intervening years by restricting cell lines, and then, in 2006, to veto any chance of rescuing the research under the current policy. But did he ever truly have his bearings on the issues? In twenty years of in vitro fertilization, he voiced no public concerns, yet he promoted adoption of excess embryos, as if he had stumbled upon the problem and its solution on the same day. I am lost as to how he navigated through that inconsistency to the moral high ground from which he declaims that a cluster of cells created outside of a womb, smaller than this (.), discarded as waste, is of greater value than your daughter, your son, your spouse, your mother, your father, your brother, your sister, your cousin, your grandparents—or you.

We've been blessed with the resources, the intelligence, spirit, and the energy to tackle these kinds of problems and we're all set to do it . . . Since when does America wait for someone else to figure it out?

I don't know for a fact that stem cell research has the answers to our medical miseries. In the early 1960s, nobody knew for a fact that we'd land a man on the surface of the moon within a decade. As Chris Reeve would say, "President Kennedy based his hopes on knowledge, and the projection of where that knowledge can take us." NASA pulled off what only years earlier was sci-fi fantasy, in part, due to "a willingness not to buy into the conventional wisdom." Our hope for where stem cells can take us is informed by the collective knowledge of the nation's most brilliant medical scientists and researchers. Based on that knowledge, the hope is shared by a majority of America's citizens and endorsed by both houses of Congress. Conventional wisdom finally bought into us. No one else on our side was going to get two minutes of airtime to speak up, to voice our hope and our frustration.

If I can add my voice, and for whatever reason, get a little more attention, I'm happy to do it.

The High Road to the Campaign Trail

NEW YORK CITY · SEPTEMBER/OCTOBER 2006

Campaign headquarters were in my Upper East Side office on the ground floor of our co-op. Though intrinsic to the building, the office can't be accessed from within. I have to get dressed, brave the elements, and commute approximately one hundred steps out of the lobby doors, around the corner, and into the side street door. It last served as a doctor's office, but I've never known the nature of the practice. Apparently, patients didn't need frequent treatment, because in the seven years since the doc closed shop a few would still occasionally show up at my door, unaware that he was gone. They never seemed all that surprised to see me, which tells you something.

It was Debi Brooks, the talented former Goldman Sachs vice president and cofounder of the Fox Foundation, who suggested John Rogers for this campaign mission. A singular strategist and visionary in her own right, Debi's focus over the last six years had been revolutionizing the link between science and philanthropy. Having built something extraordinary at the foundation, she was wisely protective. Our organization doesn't receive any federal funding, so there were no looming conflicts of the sort Chris grappled with during the 2004 election. However, she cautioned that the foundation couldn't operate as a middleman or facilitator in any campaign enterprise, or it risked losing tax-exempt status. Moreover, for our donors, supporting our work shouldn't mean signing on to a political agenda with which they might disagree. The foundation is about promoting and financing advances in Parkinson's research, first, foremost, fully, and finally. Any politics needed to be on my own time, at my own expense, and under my own name.

I sent out letters to board members and contributors, explaining my intentions, and requesting their indulgence and understanding. One of our most generous contributors, the chairman of a highly successful chain of family restaurants, well known for his support of the Republicans, fired back an expletive-filled missive, denouncing my efforts with every anti-liberal epithet imaginable. I barely made it to his sincerely warm sign-off wherein he tipped the joke and pledged to continue his support beyond the millions he had already given.

In touch by phone in August, John and I were equal parts vexed and motivated by the President's veto and fired up to help effect a policy change at long last. Historically, my efforts in advocating stem cell research had been reactive and defensive in nature; a candidate or coalition would contact me, or I'd respond strictly to a media inquiry, as opposed to engaging them with ideas and questions of my own. Under the aegis of John and his team, we would turn the old MO on its head. I'd be proactive, interjecting myself directly into the political discourse—going on offense.

Shambling into my Manhattan office on September 14, John found me well oriented in the terrain of the 2006 midterm election landscape. The next couple of hours were dedicated to defining what we intended to do in the next few weeks. In broad terms, we were seeking a shift in the balance of power, not from Republican to Democrat, but from anti–stem cell to pro–stem cell. A majority of Congress was already on board, but we needed to secure a veto-proof two-thirds margin. To avoid confusing and thereby diminishing our message, we would be a one-issue operation. The war in Iraq, Katrina, the congressional scandals, education, immigration, and prescriptions for the economy, we'd leave to others. We were going to avoid "politics as usual" altogether and, rather than dividing voters with a "wedge issue," set out to unite people over the promise of stem cell research.

How could we help bring about this shift? We'd find races where an anti–stem cell candidate or incumbent opposed a pro–stem cell candidate or incumbent. It didn't matter which was Democrat or Republican, so long as they disagreed. A thorough survey, however, uncovered no pro–stem cell Republicans opposing anti–stem cell Democrats. I had, in the 2004 Republican primary, supported Arlen Specter when his pro stance came under attack, and I remained willing to help any proponent, unless he or she favored invading Canada or other untenable agendas.

We agreed to get involved only in close races, and where we were wanted and could make a positive difference.

During a midterm election everything but the presidency is up for grabs: municipal races, state legislatures, gubernatorial races, the House, and the Senate. After circling around it, we finally made what in hindsight was a key decision. We committed to some pivotal House races, and at least one close (and symbolic) governor's race held interest, but we intuitively gravitated toward the Senate. True, Senate races had a higher profile, but conventional wisdom didn't favor the Democrats to win the Senate, despite a raft of Democratic Senate candidates that would impress even a Republican. Missouri's Claire McCaskill, Maryland's Ben Cardin, and Virginia's Jim Webb were accomplished individuals from varied backgrounds, bona fide supporters of stem cell research, and on the record with their critiques of the current policy.

Of the Senate races, one in particular fired our imaginations: Claire McCaskill challenging Jim Talent for his Missouri Senate seat. Stem cells had become a lightning rod in Missouri, a state with nearly equal parts religious conservatives and urban progressives. They would also be voting on a stem cell ballot initiative similar to Prop 71 that passed in California in 2004, a measure to promote and fund stem cell research in the state. Missouri's measure was somewhat more controversial as it endorsed somatic nuclear cell transfer (therapeutic cloning).

The governor's race in Wisconsin also presented an excellent chance to make a tangible difference. I had visited with Jim Doyle both in New York and Wisconsin. Tremendously proud of Wisconsin's leading role in the development of embryonic stem cells, Governor Doyle justifiably boasts of its universities, facilities, institutions, and its scientific pioneers like James Thomson, credited as the father of American stem cell research. Governor Doyle's opponent, Mark Green, wanted nothing less than a complete ban on the science. As I stood with him one November morning at a Milwaukee campaign stop, the governor warned voters, "If you elect my opponent, four years from now, we'll be saying, 'What have we done?' with very little room for 'What can we do now?' It'll be moot, the ship will have sailed, and there will be no more of this cutting-edge research in Wisconsin."

John jotted down a list of states and slid it to me across the table like a lawyer at a settlement negotiation: NJ, OH, MO, VA, MD, MI, WI, RI, MN, and MT. Those who by their own assessment met our criteria quickly welcomed our help. Case in point: Richard Martin, Claire McCaskill's campaign manager in Missouri, immediately called to express enthusiasm, seeing my involvement as a natural fit for them. Their candidate was neck-and-neck with Senator Talent, and stem cell research was emerging as one of the big issues. Since this was arguably the pivotal race in the nation, we were itching to help.

McCaskill gave us our first chance to field test what I would and wouldn't do. No to press conferences and, for reasons purely having to do with my unpredictable windows of articulate speech and motor function, no to debates. TV ads could work (*we had no idea just how well*), and events with a moderate amount of speechifying would be fine. We also agreed to endorsements via press release when a stop in a candidate's home turf was not doable.

October 5, 2006, marked our first steps onto the campaign trail, and we vowed to stick to the high road. Looking back, the high road now evokes an image of Wile E. Coyote, zipping around a blind curve on a steep, winding mountain pass, to find himself improbably suspended in midair, cycling his legs frantically until, resigned to his fate, he lets them dangle, waves buh-bye, and plummets to the desert floor. He always stirred up a mini mushroom cloud of dust, but survived. I had a similar adventure in store.

I arrived in a St. Louis rife with anticipation. They had pulled ahead early, and there was no looking back. The betting forecast allowed for no possibility but victory in the coming weeks. And sure enough, that evening the St. Louis Cardinals would beat San Diego for the second game in a row, though they would need four to get past the Padres and into the World Series. In the McCaskill organization, passions for their candidate's prospects were as high as those for the Red Birds.

Just as it would be in Columbus, the unseasonable warmth threatened to undo me. I sat for interviews right there at the airport, my button-down shirt soaked through to the skin—a local print reporter first, then the TV news, and then another paper. Though I was damp and cranky, the tone was cordial in all three, and the journalists were prepared and informed, reflecting the import of stem cells in Missouri politics. My "Show-Me State" media baptism complete, I toweled off and changed into a spare shirt that my assistant, Jackie "Radar" Hamada, had been prescient enough to pack. From there it was on to a St. Louis restaurant for a McCaskill fund-raiser.

I have a new appreciation for the term "backroom politics," as my whirlwind tour, beginning in St. Louis, would entail waiting and meeting in a succession of back rooms across the country. It was in this particular St. Louis back room, the restaurant's well-stocked wine cellar, that I met candidate McCaskill and her husband, Joe. A former state representative, Jackson County prosecutor, and state auditor, Claire exuded the tough confidence and intelligence those roles require, balanced by the affability and humor necessary to survive in politics. She was well versed, and spoke fluent "Stem Cell."

I accompanied Claire into a larger room to meet and greet supporters, and then she preceded me into an even larger room for the rally. After a brief but gracious introduction, Claire called me to join her onstage. I felt comfortable and engaged, though the news footage shows obvious symptoms.

Story of my life these days: I don't always know that I'm shaking unless someone tells me (so if I'm spilling coffee on your suit, speak up). Claire articulated the promise of stem cell research and her commitment to fight for it, regardless of the political push-back. I could see that we had real allies out there. This was my first event, and I had no set patter or pre-packaged message. Rattling around in my mind, though, were two time-tested political axioms: "As goes Missouri, so goes the nation," and from the gospel according to former Speaker of the House Tip O'Neill, "All politics is local." Risking sacrilege, I amended Tip's maxim:

> In this case, in this election, in this state, and on this
> issue, all politics is *not* local. What you do here in
> Missouri has an impact on the entire country, on me,
> my wife and my four children, and all those Americans
> who either have, or love someone who has, an incurable
> disease or condition. That's what brings me to Missouri.
> It only seems fitting to say that on Election Day, if you
> care about the future, show me, show the country,
> show the world.

My first stump speech found me glancing at Claire for a nod of approval and, instead, being awarded with a bear hug.

"John says you might do an ad for us."

"Why not?" I answered.

Heading for the exit, I turned back for a parting wave to the crowd and slipped out into the last rays of a fading St. Louis afternoon. The heat wasn't fading, though, and I was all out of shirts.

Ad hom·i·nem (hom'ə·nem')

adj. Appealing to personal considerations
rather than to logic or reason.

A few days before the campaign ads I'd made for Claire Mc-
Caskill, Ben Cardin, and Jim Doyle were released, each campaign sent John Rogers their final edits to forward along to
me for my perusal and approval. Discovering them in my in-
box, I hesitated before downloading and gave John a call at his
office in Milwaukee, Wisconsin.

"What did you think?" I asked. "Did you watch all of
them?"

"They're great, pal," he replied. "Everybody's lovin' them.
Richard Martin from the McCaskill camp says it's the most
extraordinary ad he's ever been involved with. The focus
group numbers they're pulling in are through the roof!"

Extraordinary? The ads were professional and well shot with
tight, solidly factual scripts, but I personally didn't find them all
that extraordinary. Change the names involved, switch sports
coats, subtract a few wrinkles, and these were essentially iden-
tical to the ads I cut in 2004 for Specter and Kerry. *What was
different this time?* The message and the call to action were perhaps more urgent two years down the line. I quickly opened
the files to see what they'd added post-production—some kind
of special effect?

Only after multiple viewings did I understand that the special effect was me. Steven Spielberg, who is familiar with both
special effects *and* me, later told *Time* magazine that "the ads

equated the conservatives' war on science with terrible human consequences." In other words, it wasn't only what I was saying but what my body, my hands, my legs, my feet, and my eyes were doing as I said it. I have grown so used to living with the disease that I am able to direct the majority of my focus, apart from the foundation, advocacy, and general maintenance, on living and not the disease. My tremors and dyskinesias, fluid and changing, are so integrated into my daily continuum that it would be impossible to trap one moment under glass as a comprehensive representation of my condition or the condition of all Parkinson's patients. When you film a thirty-second ad, however, that's what you get—those thirty seconds of time. Only capturing one second at a time of every hour over thirty days would provide an accurate picture. When people ask me how I'm feeling, I tend to say, "Okay, but it's like the weather in New England, wait a second, and it'll change." And some, having caught that moment in a jar, so to speak, were intensely scrutinizing it, holding it up to the light, giving it a good shake, and definitely not punching any air holes into the lid.

WALDORF ASTORIA HOTEL, NEW YORK CITY
OCTOBER 18, 2006

Campaigns often complain that cash is tough to raise, but on the day we made the McCaskill, Cardin, and Doyle ads, I saw how easy it is to spend. To be fair, studio space in Manhattan is rare and priced accordingly, but for our purposes, renting one of the Waldorf Astoria's larger suites could hardly be called scrimping. Adding in the cost of the crew, three directors, and the price of airtime, the total hit had to be substantial. Looking back now, though, they got a lot of bang for their buck.

Visiting New York from Vancouver, Canada, my mother accompanied me to the Waldorf. Mom's in her mid-seventies, and I'm in my mid-forties, but that day triggered her maternal alarm, an echo from a hockey rink in Canada thirty-five years earlier, when she, in her mid-forties, watched her ten-year-old son being helped off the ice, dazed and bleeding from a stick across the face. Today she was watching that same boy, a grown man now, struggle to simply sit still in a chair. "Parents are supposed to be able to fix their children's problems," she told me. "I know you're not a child anymore, but you're my child, and I can't help you. When you volunteered to sit on your hands, I knew I was gonna lose it." Indeed, there was nothing she could do.

If you've ever played a drunken game of Whac-a-Mole, you've experienced frustration commensurate with attempting to control advanced Parkinson's symptoms. Even with careful strategy and meticulous timing, it's hit-or-miss. Or worse, it can be both.

We made the left off Park Avenue, then the quick right into the Waldorf Astoria's valet parking lane. I stepped from the car, and the moment my shoes hit the curb, my drugs kicked in. I smiled. My timing was so good, it was Swiss. The metaphorical "mole" had been whacked; the tremors and stiffness should have been neutralized for the next hour or two, but a blast of dyskinesias soon hit my brain and body. An easy technical explanation, like "overmedicated," would actually be a misnomer. An indeterminate amount of dopamine is always present in the blood and brain, even in a Parkinson's patient. The prescribed dose at the recommended time is no guarantee against side effects. For the rest of the shoot I would be in the literal sway of levodopa's side effects: the rocking, dipping, and diving of dyskinesias.

Before I had Parkinson's, I assumed tremors were the essential feature of the condition, when it is actually a paucity of movement, due to the brain's diminishing production of the neurotransmitter dopamine. Bradykinesia, with its quick shuffling steps, uncontrolled momentum, lack of any swing to the arms, and overall kinetic limitation, is the manifestation of this shortage. An apt comparison is dopamine to motor oil—critical for smooth operation. Decrease the quantity, and the engine falters and then seizes up entirely. Just as I, without dopamine, will become a-kinetic.

Each patient exhibits his or her unique combination of symptoms. Most, however, have one thing in common. Over time, levodopa loses its efficacy; patients increase their dosage until uncontrollable dyskinesias force them to accept that they've outlived its usefulness. In my eighteen years since diagnosis, I have remained so responsive to the drug that I've never had to increase dosage. Even so, dyskinesias have become pervasive.

I come at this dilemma from two directions, pharmaceutically and philosophically. At this point, philosophy often provides a more reliable remedy. Here's the choice. Pick your poison, or more accurately, pick your kinesia: bradykinesia or dyskinesia. You can be one of two people, each seated in a chair in the middle of a room. The distance to the door is about fifteen paces. For an unmedicated PD patient dealing with bradykinesia, moving forward in a straight line, provided that patient can rise from the chair, may take as many as fifty halting, shuffling steps and an indeterminate amount of time to reach the exit. And once there, he or she may not be able to execute the near impossible twist of the wrist to turn the knob. The other, profoundly dyskinetic patient may also take as many as fifty steps, but a cattle prod couldn't force him or her to follow a straight line. These steps are rapid, wide, and looping, with a dramatic lurching from side to side corrected by the occasional backward step (think "Monty Python's Ministry of Silly Walks"). The trip may take the dyskinetic patient to each corner of the room and into contact with every wall and windowsill before he or she reaches the door, takes several stabs at the doorknob, finally finds purchase, and flings it open. Absent a "None of the Above" box to tick, which of the two dilemmas would you rather face?

We Parkinson's patients, save for those increasingly elusive "on" periods when the drugs are working and the symptoms are under control, can be both of those people, alternating realities several times a day. If I have to settle, however, I'll take dyskinesias. A few misadventurous footfalls, bruising and cutting my shins on chair legs, my head rolling around like a beach ball on a boat deck—it's all a small price to pay for reaching the door and opening it with a fresh hope for what may be on the other side. Having set my mind to a task, it matters little to me what sort of interpretive dance I have to perform first. I'm just happy to be able to walk, talk, sit, and stand, albeit with the extra body English of dyskinesias. Often, as I did that day at the Waldorf, I forget the package I am presenting to the outside world. I have also learned to be resourceful and make adjustments.

In a situation like the ad shoot, when all I have to do is sit and read words from a teleprompter, a good chair is imperative. Rolling ball-wheel, swivel-type office models are a menace—they'd need a Steadicam to track me as I careened around the room. My shifting and writhing would elicit complaining shrieks from a wood-and-canvas director's chair. An armless parlor chair couldn't contain me—I'd eventually spill sideways out of frame and onto the floor. A stool is out of the question, and a spinning bar stool is potential suicide. Give me a good, solid, hardwood dining room chair, like I had at the Waldorf, with sturdy legs and arms that feature easy-to-grip hand pommels. The actual seat, its features and contours, are irrelevant. In the throes of dyskinesias, my body's energy doesn't settle into the chair but surges to its five extremities—hands, feet, and head. Hands don't rest on the pommels as much as throttle them, and feet hook around the bottom of the chair legs, anchoring my shins and calves, which, were they boneless, would wrap around the chair legs like the asp of a caduceus around its sword. With these four control factors in play, there's little ass-to-seat cushion contact, so I would billow out like a sail, if not for the gyroscopic correction of the head-bobble. There's only one answer for this. Sitting on my hands reins in excess head movement. (This is the offer I made to the cameraman that, unbeknownst to me, sent my mother fleeing from the room.)

Again, these adjustments are often unconscious. I don't give much thought to how others perceive symptoms; I have enough on my plate. I will take time, however, to explain myself to young kids, who are often curious and wonderfully straightforward. I was once talking with a little girl at Esmé's preschool, who broke off our conversation mid-sentence and exclaimed in honest exasperation, "Will you quit moving around!" I eventually managed to stop laughing long enough to promise her I'd give it a shot.

Our foundation sponsored a poker tournament, inspired by one of our board members, David Einhorn, who finished seventeenth at the 2006 World Series of Poker in Las Vegas (and donated his $660,000 purse to our work). Our small New York event had two hundred and forty players. I overachieved, finishing thirtieth, crediting my unlikely poker success to my opponents' inability to get a read on me. My whole body was one continuous, baffling tell. I would blink or widen my eyes, wiggle, nod, and shift, whether I had a three-seven unsuited or pocket aces.

Only a few nights later, however, my dyskinesias inspired a less benign confusion. Tracy and I were having sushi in Midtown. Rocking and moving to a degree that eating was impossible and knocking over the table was likely, I told Tracy I had to step outside. "Finish your meal and have mine wrapped to go," I suggested. Dramatically dyskinetic, I paced back and forth outside in a misting rain over a length of fifty or sixty feet just to the left of the restaurant's entrance. With a sweeping limp, one arm across my chest to hold the other in check, and my head nodding like a davening rabbi, every thirty seconds or so I paused to lean against a graffitied brick wall. The few pass-ersby threw uncomfortable glances and quickened their pace. None too comfortable myself, I offered little acknowledgment, but even after they passed, I felt scrutinized. An awkward, owl-ish sweep of the block confirmed my intuition when I spotted a guy loitering in a doorway across the street, eyeballing me bla-tantly and without apology. I checked my watch for the ninth or tenth time and considered my options. Rejoining Tracy was out; my symptoms were too big and the confines of the restau-rant too small to wend through feng shui table placements and tell her I was going home. I rarely carry a cell phone, so I couldn't call her, and besides, with these dyskinesias, I'd proba-bly dial Kuala Lumpur. Mr. Doorway, sensing my imminent departure, made his move. He crossed the street, halted about a foot away, and continued to stare. I stared back, but with my head swaying, I was hardly at my New York badass best.

"You waiting for someone?" he asked, his voice just above a whisper, eyes a little loose in their sockets. "Who do you usu-ally see around here?" He squinted, bit his lip, and then was all business. "You looking to buy?" he asked.

Every episode of *The Wire* I'd ever watched kicked in, and I suddenly got it. From my erratic movement and watch-auditing, he'd pegged me as a junkie looking to score. Mo-mentarily stumped for an answer, I finally settled on the kid-tested, mother-approved "Fuck off."

"Hey," he said, hands up in a calming gesture. "It's all right, I'm not a cop."

I was ready with my reply, "Oh . . . Okay . . . So fuck off!"

After watching him lope away, I finally went back into the

restaurant, found Tracy just paying the bill, and told her, by the way, that should she be wanting a heroin aperitif, I knew a guy.

CHICAGO, ILLINOIS · OCTOBER 24, 2006

Choosing to invest time, energy, and identity in the political process is an expression of hope. If something in our personal experience has informed or inspired us to believe that one direction or outcome is preferable to another, for not only the individual, but society as a whole, we put that belief into action through activism, advocacy, financial support of a candidate, actually running for office, or by simply casting a vote. The American political experience can therefore be viewed as optimism in the collective. Naturally, unanimity is rare, as reasonable (and not so reasonable) people are bound to disagree. Take it from me, things get a little intense when the swords come out and all you're holding is a plowshare.

When I first felt the jab of the swords, Jackie and I had just arrived in Chicago on the morning flight out of New York. We were to head directly to a campaign appearance on behalf of Major Tammy Duckworth, a Democrat hoping to win Henry Hyde's soon-to-be-vacant seat in the staunchly conservative sixth congressional district outside Chicago. The plan was to stay over Tuesday night, attend an unrelated nonpolitical donor luncheon for the Michael J. Fox Foundation, and then return to New York Wednesday afternoon. As we deplaned, we were met by John Rogers, Kelly Boyle, and Alan McLeod. Throughout our handshakes and hellos, the three of them were like multimedia jugglers, responding to the cacophony of buzzes, trills, and ring tones emanating from their cell phones, BlackBerrys, and other various PDAs. Now off the plane, Jackie had activated hers as well, and instantly, it began clamoring for her attention. From the look on everyone's face, the urgent tone of their whispered questions and answers, and the furious flurry of their text messaging, it was obvious that some serious shit was in the wind.

We met up with a Duckworth staffer who led us to yet another rented campaign minivan. Hustling through the parking lot, John briefed me on the situation. There had been a conservative response to the campaign ads, the Mc-Caskill ad in particular. We had anticipated this, but what we hadn't counted on was that no less an attack dog than Rush Limbaugh, conservative radio talk show host and political commentator, was leading the charge. Much of his previous day's broadcast had been devoted to not so much debunking the ad on its merits or plumbing the ethical complexities of stem cell research, but going after me specifically ad hominem and apparently ad nauseam. Up to this point, I had been completely unaware—my radio tastes tend toward classic rock and NPR. He'd been going on about it since the first McCaskill ad interrupted game one of the World Series, while he was no doubt enjoying his hometown Cardinals' domination of the Detroit Tigers. The gist of his complaint, I was learning from John and his staff, was that I was a faker, exaggerating, playing up, and manufacturing symptoms in order to stir sympathy and pity in the hearts and minds of voters.

"What the hell did you get me into, John?" I muttered.

John, who was sitting in the backseat of the latest campaign minivan on our way to our hotel in suburban Chicago, shrugged and said, "Well, pal, I'm not quite sure of that yet myself, but it's gonna be fun."

"For you maybe," I laughed.

"Let's just see where it goes," he said.

We poured the tepid dregs of our Starbucks coffees out of the van's windows as we pulled into the hotel parking lot. We had a busy morning ahead of us. I couldn't think of a more appropriate person than Major Tammy Duckworth to spend the morning with, given that I'd woken up to the fact that I was in for a hell of a fight. Tammy, after all, was no stranger to tough fights. Here she was, a political newcomer, a Democrat, with the guts to compete for the seat Henry Hyde was vacating in this most conservative of Chicago suburbs.

Less than two years earlier, Major Duckworth, a thirty-eight-year-old National Guard pilot, had lost both her legs in Iraq when the Black Hawk helicopter she was copiloting was hit by a rocket-propelled grenade and brought down. Ten days later she woke up in Walter Reed Army Medical Center in Washington, DC, and by August of 2005, she had decided to run for Congress. Not given a chance in the traditionally Republican district, she was now, less than two weeks before Election Day, engaged in an unexpectedly competitive race with her GOP opponent, Peter Roskam.

Before meeting with Tammy, still en route to the rally, I had the standard local interviews, one in print and one televised. My inner circle had moved from the van to a holding room within the hotel, where they would prep me for the interviews. Under normal circumstances this would involve refreshing myself on the issues of research and the point-counterpoint that developed between sides of the debate. But now there was this new element to the discussion. How to respond to Rush?

"Let me get this straight one more time. He said I did what?" I asked.

"That you were either faking your symptoms or that you purposefully didn't take your medication when you shot the ads so that your symptoms would be exaggerated," John answered.

"Wait, let's back up," I said. "Did he say anything about stem cells, about the merits of the research, or any inaccuracies in the statements we made in the ad?"

"Mostly just that you were a fraud," Kelly said. I detected a slight upturn at the corner of her mouth as she said it. *Was she actually smiling?*

"Oh," Alan joined in. "He also said you were pandering to Missouri voters by pronouncing Missouri *Missoura.*"

Then I smiled too and half-laughed as I responded, "You've gotta be kidding."

A Duckworth aide tapped on the door. The local NBC reporter was ready to do the on-camera interview in another room of the hotel.

In my role as an advocate for Parkinson's-related issues, my key responsibility is to inform and educate, to promote understanding of what we go through as individuals and as a community. For the first time that I could remember, my message was being countered by someone equally visible and even more vocal than I, and to make matters worse, he was actively and enthusiastically disseminating misinformation, promoting ignorance.

"We don't know for sure that she's gonna bring this up in the interview," John said as I put on my jacket and he instinctively straightened my tie.

"And if she does?" I asked. I mean, this stuff was almost too crazy. I decided that I'd just go with the truth, that I hadn't heard or read the exact comments yet and wasn't in a position to respond. As I was being escorted to the interview, I took stock of my physical condition. I was actually feeling pretty good this morning. My meds had kicked in nicely; my gait was smooth, my hands were steady, and as of yet, I had no pronounced dyskinesias. *Great. Or was it?*

I knew of course that to simply dismiss Limbaugh's allegations as crazy would be dangerous. If he was crazy, then he was, pardon the expression, crazy like a fox. It was a classic "when did you stop beating your wife?" provocation, based not on an accusation, but on a presumption that something sinister had been perpetrated. His diatribe had set out an array of traps for me to stumble into if I wasn't careful, the first of which lay immediately ahead.

Like I said, I was feeling good that morning. It's always the goal to be as comfortable as possible, particularly in public situations. But was there now suddenly such a thing as being too comfortable, too smooth—not symptomatic enough? I wasn't going to involve myself with circular bullshit, manufacturing symptoms to prove I wasn't manufacturing symptoms.

It turned out that the two reporters I spoke to weren't entirely up to speed on Rush's attack, so his remarks were only referred to in passing and rather obliquely at that.

The morning received a much-needed injection of class when I finally met Major Tammy Duckworth, just moments before the rally. Her warm smile and affable nature immediately put me at ease. Very quickly we were exchanging anecdotes about our respective experiences as political neophytes on the campaign trail. She was the first to mention the attention coming my way from the conservative Right; having heard Limbaugh on the radio, she found herself "in utter disbelief," though she had faced similar accusations herself. After brief inquiries about each other's health, she matter-of-factly showed me the prosthetics she wore on each leg, admitting with a smile that any height advantage she held over me, she acquired with her new prosthetic legs.

I had read Major Duckworth's campaign biographical materials and was familiar with her story. Be that as it may, meeting her was nothing short of inspirational. Her example—transforming a tragic circumstance into an opportunity for service—put into sharp relief the character of those detractors who claimed she was using her disability to evoke sympathy. I pity anyone who would make the mistake of having pity for Tammy Duckworth. She's the real deal. Even more obvious than her toughness is her positive spirit. In the first moment of eye contact, it is clear that she believes in what she's doing and has a real hope—an informed optimism—

that given the opportunity, she can affect positive change, not only for disabled vets, from whom she drew the inspiration to run, but for people in her district, her country, and the world.

Never a "super-optimistic person" before she was injured, she says, "I'm more optimistic now than I was before." She points out that battlefield triage has advanced over the last ten years to such a degree that "I would not have survived if I had been injured in the first Gulf War."

Unfortunately, advances in our ability to treat victims on the battlefield haven't been matched by our capacity to care for them once they've returned stateside, to heal and rehabilitate. Military hospitals, the Veterans Administration, the entire system, already considered by many to be woefully impersonal and inefficient, are now buckling almost to the point of breaking under the strain. Tammy discovered this firsthand in the days, weeks, and months she spent in the hospital being treated for her horrific injuries. "When I was at Walter Reed, I started doing advocacy work for other patients because I was the highest-ranking amputee there for a while," she told me. "So whenever anyone needed to speak as a representative for other patients, they sent me. I started talking about the bureaucracy that existed and how we need to get rid of it. I testified before the Senate and the House, and through that process I was sucked into being politically active even though I never was before. The army had assigned me to this post for the other patients and then I started calling Senator Durbin's office saying, look, we've got a problem here or a problem there, I need help. It was in the late summer when Senator Durbin called me and told me that if I'm this upset about things that are not happening, I should run for office. At that point he mentioned Henry Hyde's district to me."

The rally was held in one of the hotel's large banquet halls. The room was already packed and raucous with cheering and chanting as we entered, gauntlet-style, the Major proceeding through a phalanx of well-wishers and supporters on either side. It was hard to grasp what any individual was saying, but suffice it to say, I was hearing the name "Rush" a lot, usually accompanied by an expletive or two. Metal risers accommodated the media, which was out in force—a dozen or so TV cameras and two or three times as many still photographers. I kept my comments brief, with most of the focus on Tammy and stem cell research. As with the two interviews I had done earlier, I didn't mention Rush Limbaugh specifically. In fact, from that point on, with only one exception, I didn't say the guy's name in any public forum for the remainder of the campaign. I couldn't help but appreciate the enormous roar of approval when I made a passing reference to a certain "less than compassionate conservative" who had spoken out against our efforts. It was a good line, and I'd keep using it for the next two weeks.

That afternoon I checked into a hotel in downtown Chicago; I had a luncheon the next day for some Fox Foundation donors in the Chicago area. The political portion of my junket was now complete. But of course, my mind was entirely occupied with politics.

There was no question that I was on edge. Having been retired for the most part from acting for the last few years, it had been a while since I had received a bad review, and I don't think I'd ever heard one so surgically personal in nature. This was not disagreement, disapproval, or even distaste. This was disgust, that same sort of sharp rebuke I had seen dealt out to those over the past few years who had spoken out against government policy, although their comments had largely been about the war and the administration's actions leading up to it. I was being "Dixie Chicked."

This was new for me, and I suddenly realized how much I had always liked being liked. It is spooky to see that a contingent of society, vocal and connected to power, has worked up an antipathy toward you and is rallying this base to marginalize you and the threat you represent. Would I have still made the ads if I'd had some idea of what the stakes were for my public reputation?

Absolutely. The stakes for me as a patient and an advocate were infinitely higher. My options had been narrowed to the basic "fight or flight," and I wasn't about to run away, but I was anxious and a little unsure as to how to respond.

My immediate plan was to order some room service and watch the baseball game. While I was waiting for dinnertime to roll around, I compulsively forged through the contents of the minibar, putting a large dent in the inventory. Not the booze, of course—after fifteen years of being sober, it would take more than a gust of hot air from Rush Limbaugh to blow me off the wagon. I did, however, polish off two bags of peanut M&M's at the inflated hotel price of about eight bucks each, some gelatinous lemon wedge–type things, coated in crystallized sugar, and some salty squares with wasabi peas from a bag labeled entirely in Japanese except for the single English word "SNACK."

There were a number of phone calls. The wider media, smelling blood in the water, were circling and looking for someone to feed them something. John called to gather a statement. I told him I wasn't sure yet.

"Tell ya what, pal, for today, I'm just gonna speak on your behalf and say something general, but accurate—express shock and disappointment at the ignorance of his statements and reaffirm your commitment to continue speaking out on behalf of stem cells."

That was cool with me.

The phone rang again. It was my mom. She didn't even ask if it was me, but instead, immediately led with the question "Are you okay?"

There's a way that people ask that question, teeming with the certainty that you aren't, that makes you do a quick scan of your extremities and put the back of your hand to your forehead just to make sure that indeed, you are, before answering in the affirmative.

"What an idiot that man is. I'm so mad I can't see straight."

"Mom, it's all right."

"He's just ignorant. He has no idea what he's talking about!"

"That's why it's okay. No serious person will take him seriously."

As we talked, it became clear that what had Mom especially fired up, aside from the natural maternal instinct to defend her kid, was her recollection of the day the ads were filmed, how upset she was to see me struggle with dyskinesias.

"I didn't even know you listened to his show."

"I don't," she said. "But other people do, and they've been calling. Then I saw him imitating you on TV and I was so livid."

"You saw him doing what?" I said. This was the first I'd heard of this.

"He was imitating you, making fun of you—wiggling, shaking, squirming around."

Jesus, Hunter S. Thompson was right. When the going gets weird, the weird definitely do turn pro.

My subsequent telephone conversation with Tracy went a long way toward keeping my head in the right place. Sensibly, she was neither as angry as my mother nor as baffled as I still seemed to be.

"Congratulations," she said. "You got their attention."

Tracy, as she so often does, had hit the nail on the head. I had the attention not only of Rush Limbaugh and his "ditto heads," but also of those in the media and general public drawn to the sound of their complaints. The attention had created an opportunity to educate. I'd have to give a little more thought as to how best to capitalize on that opportunity. In the meantime, John's first public comment on my behalf was a step in the right direction: "It's a shameful statement. It's appallingly sad that people who don't understand Parkinson's disease feel compelled to make these comments. Anyone who understands the disease knows that it is because of the medications that Parkinson's sufferers experience dyskinesias."

That next morning, I had some time to kill before my only

remaining responsibility in the Chicago area—that luncheon sponsored by the foundation for local supporters and researchers. The *New York Times* crossword puzzle seemed like a reasonable distraction, so I opened up the Arts and Leisure section. Scanning for the traditional black-and-white grid, my eyes fell upon a column by Alessandra Stanley, the *Times* television critic. Her review of our ad, under the headline "Making Stem Cell Issue Personal, and Political," was reasoned and insightful. Even after reading just the first paragraph, I had a fuller understanding of the emotions we had tapped into on both sides of the issue, from Richard Martin and his popcorn polls to Limbaugh and the ditto heads.

> The plea is as disturbing—and arresting—as a hostage video from Iraq. In a navy blazer and preppy Oxford shirt, the actor Michael J. Fox calmly asks viewers to support stem cell research by voting for several Democratic candidates in Maryland, Missouri, and Wisconsin, while his body sways back and forth uncontrollably like a sailor being tossed around in a full-force gale.
>
> In short, Mr. Fox's display of the toll Parkinson's disease has taken on him turned into one of the most powerful and talked about political advertisements in years.

I was slack-jawed when I finally caught the video of the Limbaugh show before I left Chicago. He flapped his arms and wiggled his fingers while rocking his body, rolling his shoulders, and bobbing his head.

[Michael J. Fox] is exaggerating the effects of the disease. He's moving all around and shaking and it's purely an act . . . This is really shameless of Michael J. Fox. Either he didn't take his medication or he's acting.

If his intention was only to mimic and mock what he maintained was my "shameless" performance, it went well beyond the personal—caricaturing the thousands of Parkinson's patients I'd met and worked with over the years. I saw it as an affront to them and their families, and I felt an obligation to defend them.

Predictably, my reception at the luncheon for the foundation was warm and supportive. Up to now, most of my focus had been on the extent to which Limbaugh and the Right had denounced the ads and the motive behind my involvement in them, but now I was getting a dose of the other side. The pro-research and patient communities were shocked and disgusted by the political attack. On the plane back home and at the airports on both ends of my journey, I discovered that my well-wishers extended beyond those with an interest in Parkinson's or stem cells. At the check-in counter, through security, and at the baggage claim, people approached me with words of encouragement. The consistent message I was getting was that I should fight back. While I appreciated the sentiment, I was wary of letting myself be distracted and engaging in the wrong fight. My battle was not with a conservative radio talk show host, whose intention among other things was to distract me and others from our message, but rather, against those in power who willfully sought to impede the progress of scientific research that could improve the lives of millions.

Limbaugh wasn't alone in his objections to the ads and my participation in them. Predictably, representatives of the candidates whose anti–stem cell views I was effectively campaigning against took issue with our message; but what they had no way around was the indisputable effects and ravages of catastrophic illness. It's ironic that one answer for it could very well be the research they so strongly opposed.

Over the course of the few hours that it took to travel back from Chicago to New York, the controversy only intensified. Limbaugh apparently was feeling the force of a backlash. His allegation that I had been manufacturing symptoms to manipulate voters had been effectively countered by John's explanation about dyskinesias. Originally Limbaugh had pointed to the fact that in my first book I mentioned my first testimony before Congress when I chose not to take my Sinemet (levodopa) so that the impaneled legislators could see the full, unmodified effects of the disease. Limbaugh brandished this detail as if it were a smoking gun, but his logic was flawed. As Stanley explained in her *Times* article, "If Mr. Fox did forgo medication for the advertisement as Mr. Limbaugh suggested, it could hardly be considered fraudulent: if anything, masking the extent of the disease's ravages is the deception, not revealing them."

Slightly chastened, Limbaugh allowed that he would "bigly, hugely, admit that I was wrong, and I will apologize to Michael J. Fox if I am wrong in characterizing his behavior in this commercial as an act." Surprisingly, perhaps benefiting from low expectations in general, this was widely regarded as an apology from the talk show host, or as close as he was going to get to one.

His next salvo was, I think, intended to work on two levels. Having already alluded to my being an actor and, therefore, a con man, he now made the next logical connection. If my being an actor didn't necessarily mean that I was faking my symptoms, it was a pretty safe bet that I was a liberal and, therefore, a de facto Democrat. He went on to say, "Michael J. Fox is allowing his illness to be exploited and in the process is shilling for a Democratic politician."

Friends and associates from every corner of my life—professional, personal, and medical—were quick to correct him at every turn, loudly and convincingly. Moreover, members of the media were themselves having fun poking holes in his accusations. Left-leaning MSNBC commentator Keith Olbermann took glee in responding to the Democratic "shill" comment by pointing out that I had, in fact, supported and campaigned on behalf of pro-stem cell Republicans in the past.

What I needed to do, I decided, more than anything else, was to seize the opportunity that had presented itself, to use this spotlight that had been fixed upon me right up to Election Day. The only acceptable counter to all of this negativity was positivity.

Late in the evening after I returned from Chicago, Tracy found me standing at the fridge, door open, staring vacantly at a jar of mayonnaise, as men are wont to do. Intuiting that I wasn't really looking for anything but just filling the moment with an instinctive activity, she gently closed the door and pulled me in for a hug.

"You must be exhausted," she said.

"Yeah, I guess so," I replied. "But I feel really calm, ya know? This whole thing, the ads, Limbaugh, stem cells, the elections—it's like a perfect storm. And I'm right in the center of it, the eye, I mean. I just feel so weirdly relaxed."

"I know. It's great," she said. "I think this is the first time since I've known you that you haven't worried about pissing anybody off. You're always such a diplomat. But when it comes to this, you have such conviction, you truly don't give a shit about what anybody thinks—especially Rush Limbaugh."

"I care what you think," I said.

"I think you should get some sleep."

Good thinking.

. . .

My physical condition drew attention to the human cost of a failure to pursue breakthroughs in scientific research, just as Tammy Duckworth's injuries pointed to the price some were paying for our decision to go to war. However articulate we are in expressing our positions, it is the unspoken part of our message, over which we have no control, that is irrefutable and therefore extremely frustrating to our critics. Don't want people to be reminded of the terrible toll of war? Don't let the media show images of flag-draped coffins returning from Iraq, and characterize any critical examination of the war as unpatriotic.

It had taken me a long time to get past the idea that my symptoms and physical challenges were offensive to me, but I had never truly given much thought to the prospect that they might be offensive to anyone else. So how to process that?

In a recently published *New York Times* article, "Clearly, Frankly, Unabashedly Disabled," Mireya Navaro asserts that "the public image of people with disabilities," which "often hinged on the heroic or the tragic," is changing. Interviewed for the piece, actor and double amputee Robert David Hall, who plays a coroner on the CBS series *CSI*, observed, "It used to be that if you were disabled and on television, they'd play soft piano music behind you." I particularly like this observation because it gives a real insight into the packaging that people feel is necessary when presenting images of stories about the people we refer to as disabled. At once the same and the opposite of the shrieking violins in the shower scene of *Psycho,* it roots our reaction to what we are seeing away from thinking and directly toward emotion. The right score under the image of an attack dog could convince us we're looking at a puppy. It's dehumanizing and marginalizing and it's easy to see why, as Ms. Navaro in the *Times* points out, people like Robert David Hall speak out. If society is encouraged to view you in a certain way, you come with theme music not of your choosing and perhaps not suited to your point of view. It's something you have to overcome with each encounter and experience. Why is this segment of the population responsible not only for how they feel, but how *you* feel about how they feel?

The *Times* article quotes Kaylee Haddad, an amputee who'd been approached by a mother at a neighborhood pool who told her to put her prosthetic leg back on because it was "upsetting my child." The only explanation, if not excuse, for the thoughtlessness of this mother is fear. Unwilling or unable to explain disabilities to her daughter, she reacts to Ms. Haddad as though she were the transgressor. Yet it seems ridiculous to imagine a mother approaching an able-bodied woman at a pool and asking her to drape a towel over one of her legs because it's upsetting her amputee daughter.

NEW YORK CITY · OCTOBER 26, 2006

Wanting me to slam Rush Limbaugh, preferably on their air, requests ran the gamut from talk radio shows—liberal and conservative—to the seeming thousands of cable news programs. Two names that stood out on the list of potential interviewers were Katie Couric and George Stephanopoulos. I have already mentioned George, and besides having been interviewed many times by Katie when she was on *The Today Show,* we live in the same neighborhood and often pass each other as we walk our kids to the bus stop on school-day mornings. I wouldn't characterize either as a close friend, but I knew that they would be intelligent and fair, and were informed on stem cell research.

I'm old enough to remember Walter Cronkite, dean of news anchormen and the most trusted man in America (he had a pretty solid rep in Canada too), so stepping onto the set of the *CBS Evening News* in midtown Manhattan gained me a further appreciation for the history and tradition of the institution. I heard Katie's voice, and turned as she approached to welcome me. I could sense the enormity of the weight that had been placed upon this diminutive but determined broadcaster. I understood that I was the day's hot topic and therefore a good "get," but what Katie and her producers had proposed was extraordinary, the first seven and last six minutes of their broadcast. While we did have a personal connection, I was prepared for her to be as tough as she needed to be.

As if to confirm this, in the seconds before tape rolled—the floor director literally counting down—Katie leaned toward me and quietly allowed, "Now I have to forget how much I like you." After opening remarks to the camera, she turned to me, polite but professional, and asked, "How are you?"

Let's see. I was already sweating; my assistant, Jackie, had talked me into a sports coat over a blue cashmere sweater over a T-shirt. My fashion deference to the women in my life, dating back to Mom laying out clothes at the end of my bed, prevented me from protesting that we were in the middle of a heat wave. Now, under the studio lights, aesthetics became less important than absorbency. Shaking uncontrollably, I sought in vain to establish and maintain a single, consistent physical attitude, like a gate swinging in the wind, waiting for the latch to catch. Partly at my urging, partly on its own initiative, my right arm, in a semi-controlled flail, tried to catch and contain my left leg, the ankle of which crossed my right knee. And I knew that if my hand wasn't there to police it, a violent spasm could cause a painful kick to Katie's shin. If this was distracting to her, she didn't let on. I was also occupied by what I call a "central body tremor"; it feels as though someone has punched through my torso, grabbed ahold of my spine, and is waving me like a flag.

"I'm fine, thank you."

Katie began asking about symptoms, allowing a chance to correct the mistaken ideas and address willful ignorance. It took four questions for Katie to invoke Limbaugh's name and his allegations of fakery. She played the role of devil's advocate, albeit a more polite version, in deference to the sensibilities of others, putting Limbaugh's attack in more reasonable terms.

"Could you have waited to do that ad when you had less dyskinesias, for example?"

My answer was immediate. "Well, when do you know when that's going to be? . . . It's just not that simple." I saw this as an opportunity to correctly and necessarily take it away from the personal—this was not just about me.

> That's why we're doing this. Not only people with
> Parkinson's. People who have spinal cord injuries.
> People who have the ticking clock of ALS, where they
> waste away, kids who are born with juvenile diabetes. I
> mean, potentially there's answers for those people.
> We're not interested in being exhibitionists with our
> symptoms or asking for pity or anything else. We're
> just resolved to get moving with this science. It's been a
> long time. It's not a time-neutral situation.

We moved on to explaining the disease and, more importantly, why I had chosen this moment to speak up. Aside from being the first of several high-profile interviews that I would do over the next couple of weeks, two things about the *CBS Evening News* stand out in my mind. It was my first and only time, on the campaign before or after, that I uttered Rush Limbaugh's name. (I believe the quote was "I don't give a damn about Rush Limbaugh's pity.") And the second was something Katie did later in the interview, as the drugs kicked in and the tremors segued into the jerkiness of dyskinesias. Somewhere in the contortions of making a point, my left arm detached the microphone clip from my jacket lapel. With no fuss and hardly a break in conversation or eye contact, she calmly leaned over and refastened it. Neither of us commented on it, but it was such an empathetic gesture, so far from anything patronizing or pitying, a simple kindness that allowed me the dignity to carry on making a point more important than the superficiality of my physical circumstance.

I was aware of Katie's familial connection to Parkinson's disease—her father had PD. She disclosed this information as well as her previous support for the foundation at the end of the interview. Still, it would be hard for any objective viewer to judge the exchange as anything but fair. One thing was clear though, whether or not she was able to forget how much she liked me: with that single act of consideration, she made it abundantly clear how much she loved her father.

NEW YORK CITY · OCTOBER 27, 2006

The impact of the Couric piece was immediate and powerful. My voice mail and e-mail were full. Not surprisingly, the Parkinson's and patient advocacy communities were supportive and gratified by the measured tone of our response. By neither appearing defensive nor firing back with inflammatory rhetoric, we were taking the high road, effectively a passive resistance sort of approach. In fact, Meg Ryan, an old friend of Tracy's, called her and jokingly asked, "What's it liked to be married to Gandhi?" That's me, Mahatma J. Gandhi.

The show was widely watched and the *CBS Evening News* registered a significant bump in its overnight numbers. (A recent *New York* magazine article chronicling Katie's tenure as a news anchor pointed to our segment as both a ratings and editorial highlight.) Personally, I felt a real sense of relief.

I certainly hadn't been at my best physically—I looked like shit. But it was a different kind of shit than in the ads, and most importantly, I didn't give a shit how shitty I looked. I admitted to Katie, "It's not pretty when it gets bad . . . but I've had enough years of people thinking I was pretty, and teenage girls hanging my picture on the wall. I'm over that now." Watching the playback, I was confronted by the physical price I was paying for my efforts and the certainty that it was a bargain for the privilege. The forum Katie provided, to state our position passionately yet with a calm diplomacy, provided a sharp contrast to the belligerence of those attempting to confuse the issue. It helped shift the tone.

Later that afternoon, John and I and our retinue were at ABC's Manhattan studios for the next stop on our schedule of appearances. George Stephanopoulos had flown up from his Washington base, no doubt wishing that I was still on the Vineyard. I anticipated, correctly, that George would be after the political angle more than the personal. As I endured the rituals of paint and powder in the makeup room, George and I kidded around, talking politics and family.

Physically, true to formless form, I had given up any pretense of control or calibration of symptoms and went before the cameras feeling at ease, if not anywhere close to being comfortable.

George started off with the rantings of Mr. Limbaugh. Still loose from the joviality of the backstage conversation, I went right away to the ridiculousness of Limbaugh's premise: "When I heard his response, I was like, 'What, are you kidding me?' . . . It just seemed so 'No, it can't be.'"

"But your mom was mad," George countered.

I said yes, then alluded to "the way Irish moms can get."

"Or Greek moms," he replied.

Much of the remaining conversation was nuts-and-bolts politics, detailing campaign positions, methods, and tactics. But a later reference to Limbaugh returned me to a theme that I had touched upon before and that would become a major part of my message in the coming days—the intrinsic faith we have in ourselves as Americans to do the right thing. I also touched upon how ironic it is that sometimes the greatest believers in the possibilities for the future are the very people who have cause to doubt.

"I'm going to bring up Rush Limbaugh one more time," George warned. "One of the things he says is that when you're talking about all these cures, you're giving people false hope and that it is cruel."

"Which is crueler," I responded, "to not have hope or to have hope? And it's not a false hope. It's an informed hope. But two steps forward, one step back, you know? It's a process. It's how this country was built. It's what we do. It seems to me that in the last few years, eight, ten years, we've just stopped. We've become incurious and unambitious. And hope, I mean, hope is . . ." My enthusiasm had now carried me to a patriotic reference that would make Emma Lazarus twist in her grave, ". . . I don't want to get too corny about it, but isn't that what the person in the harbor with the thing—?" I made an emphatic flourish with my arm and held aloft an imaginary torch indicating the Statue of Liberty, and then finished my point. "To characterize hope as some sort of malady or some kind of flaw of character or national weakness is, to me, really counter to what this country is about."

Even as the interview was winding down, Rush Limbaugh was in the rearview mirror. He had given us a significant push, and we were ready to take to the road. Let's face it, the whole episode, unpleasant though it may have been, was a gift in the same way that I have described Parkinson's as a gift. You suffer the blow, but you capitalize on the opportunity left open in its wake. "The notion of hiding—this is what struck a nerve. Feeling the need to hide symptoms is so key to what patients of all kinds of conditions, but particularly Parkinson's, have to face. We have to hide—don't let anybody see, don't let them think you're drunk, don't let them think you're incapable, don't let them think you're unstable, you're unsteady, you're flawed, you're devalued. Mask it. Hide it. Cover it up . . . We'd be better to take other things into account. We take our responsibility as citizens very seriously and our sense of ethics and, again, our spirituality and our participation in government, we take it very seriously. It's not made sinister by the fact that we have an affliction that may drive us down a certain path of activism."

Wrapping up, George inquired, "And you're campaigning next week?"

"Yes," I replied, "I'll be out there."

Vox Populi

NEW YORK CITY—ELECTION DAY,
NOVEMBER 7, 2006

I love voting, and not just in the broader sense of exercising my franchise and participating in representational democracy, but in a private way. In the few years since I've been a naturalized citizen, the simple act of voting has developed into an affirming personal ritual.

I wake up about an hour before the polls open, affording plenty of time for the pills to kick in. The kids, already slumped around the kitchen table, are dressed for school but barely conscious. Tracy does the short-order chef bit while I, with a page-rattling clatter, pull apart the Times, *the* Post, *the* News, *and* USA Today, *on the hunt for any last-minute news that might change the outcome of key races. Discussing politics with the kids is possible on occasion. This early in the morning, however, they'll have none of it—although they do pick up on Tracy's cues to gently tease me about my almost giddy enthusiasm to run out the door on a cold November morning. They are right to remind me that there is no reason for my urgency; on their way to school, they pass by the church that serves as our neighborhood polling place, and they know there are never any early morning crowds or lines. They're missing the point.*

Content with my slow and steady progress, I set out on the four-block walk to cast my vote with my hands tucked in the warm pockets of my fleece-lined coat. The morning rush hasn't started yet. The traffic is still sparse. The only things moving with any degree of alacrity are the red and yellow leaves, blowing across the avenue from the park and dancing ahead of me along the sidewalk. Surprisingly, I'm not the first to arrive at the polling station this morning. As I walk up the steps of the church, a couple of my neighbors, having already voted, offer a smile as they pass by and raise their arms to catch cabs to work. Inside the polling place, I'm alone again, except of course, for the senior citizen volunteers. They seem a little grumpy and put out at first, but then they look up, recognize me, break into wide grins, offer me hugs, and start arguing about who gets to show me to my booth and give me the rundown on how to cast my vote. I don't guess that everybody gets this treatment, but it would be nice if everybody did.

I even love the antiquated voting machines still employed in our district. I'm pretty well medicated by now, but my hands tremble enough that flipping the right toggles for the right candidates is a careful business, and pulling the enormous lever means that my feet have to be perfectly placed to achieve the proper balance.

Then it's done. I've dropped my pebble in the ocean, and hopefully, throughout the course of the day, millions of others will drop theirs in too. No single one of us knows which pebble causes the wave to crest, but each of us, quite rightly, believes that it might be ours; an act of faith.

On July 19, 2006, I had watched from a makeup trailer in Los Angeles as President Bush vetoed H.R. 810, the Stem Cell Research Enhancement Act. This legislation, drafted to lift the federal restriction that the President had introduced five years earlier, had passed through both the House and the Senate. The veto affected my long-term future and my immediate disposition. Disappointed and frustrated, I did some simple math; if it all came down to numbers, a shortfall of Congressional votes necessary to override a presidential veto, we in the patient community could take our case to the American people. And we did.

I had involved myself in nineteen House and Senate campaigns, and now, one hundred and eleven days later, at home in New York, I would soon learn the outcome of my efforts.

Even without the politicking, the dial on the intensity meter during this time of the year is always cranked up to eleven at our house. First there's Halloween, after which my energy level is artificially enhanced by an intake of copious amounts of candy pilfered from my children. With school now in full swing, the kids' homework burden is reaching critical mass. Esmé's birthday falls on November 3, and this year, she's announced that in keeping with the Peter Pan theme of her party, she's learning how to fly.

This too is traditionally the week when the Michael J. Fox Foundation has its annual fund-raising event in New York; we call it "A Funny Thing Happened on the Way to Cure Parkinson's." One of the greatest tasks for our foundation staff every year is securing big-name entertainment. I don't know if it can be directly attributed to my campaigning that year, but Sheryl Crow, who happens to be both politically active and, like Claire McCaskill and Rush Limbaugh, a native Missourian, enthusiastically volunteered to perform—so did Elvis Costello, Axl Rose, and Denis Leary.

Election Day was oddly anticlimactic. Whatever the outcome, I felt good about what I had done and why I had done it. There were invitations to attend victory rallies and celebrations in New York as well as in many of the cities and states in which I'd campaigned over the last few weeks. But I was tired and very happy to be home in the company of my family, with whom I'd been spending precious little time lately.

John called me throughout the day with updates on various races. It looked good for most of the candidates we had endorsed. Some were pleasant surprises. In Virginia, for example, Jim Webb was expected to pull off something of an upset. For others, however, the predictions were not as rosy. Tammy Duckworth, while coming closer to victory than anyone thought possible, would probably fall short.

After dinner that night, the girls busied themselves with homework, occasionally coming to me to ask for help. They were more happy I was home than curious as to why I'd been away so much. Sam watched some of the early returns with Tracy and me. He surprised me with the depth of his knowledge concerning the stem cell issue and the political machinations that prompted me to get involved. Unbeknownst to me, he and his friends had been keeping tabs on the Limbaugh controversy. Beyond the extent of his awareness, I was especially impressed by his remove. He was not defensive or protective, just very smart and very funny. He offered us examples of what this one said or what that one said, explained why they were hypocritical and, implicitly, how proud he was of me for pissing them off in the first place.

As the polls closed in the east, it was clear that this had been a good night for Democrats, in general, and a good night for pro–stem cell candidates, specifically. At around 11:30 P.M., Sam and Tracy went to bed. Sam had to wake up early for school, and Tracy, of course, had to wake up early to wake up Sam.

I sat alone in the living room, dark except for the soft glow of the television set, my only companion the plastic pumpkin head out of which I would occasionally fish a "fun-sized" pack of Skittles or an individually wrapped Twizzler. If I had found the majority of the day anticlimactic, these last few hours were proving to be fraught with suspense. It all came down to one Senate race. The winner would either represent a Democratic majority or, should the Republican candidate prevail, a split down the middle with Vice President Dick Cheney breaking tie votes. This was historic stuff.

It was the Missouri Senate race. It was Claire McCaskill, the first candidate for whom I campaigned, the candidate for whom I'd shot the ad that created so much controversy and incited the nationwide conversation about stem cells that we in the patient community had so long hoped for. She had been trailing throughout the day, but it had been too close to call. The television cutaways to her campaign headquarters found her aides and supporters enthusiastically optimistic, however; and sitting on my sofa back in New York, I understood why. McCaskill had fared poorly throughout much of rural Missouri—that was to be expected—but St. Louis and

Kansas City would be the last to report. When they finally did, they put her over the top.

I picked up the remote, hit the off switch, leaned back into the sofa, and closed my eyes. When I woke up in the exact same spot the next morning, I'm pretty sure I had a smile on my face.

PART THREE

Seeking Answers

Sally Fanjoy—James Labrenz

Hell Hath No Fury

For part of our summer each year, my family rents a small house in suburban Long Island, about a half mile from the beach. This is the time of summer when the kids are at camp or involved in one activity or another. Late one morning, Tracy was out on a bike ride and I was lounging on the wraparound porch reading. Hearing the crunch of footsteps on the gravel driveway, I looked up to see a youngish couple, she in a plain modest dress and he in a suit jacket and tie, making their way toward the house. I met them at the edge of the porch, knowing, of course, that they were Jehovah's Witnesses. They introduced themselves as such and handed me a *Watchtower* tract.

According to family practice and the custom of most people I've known throughout my life, my next move was supposed to be to say, "No, thanks," and close the door politely but firmly. Two things prevented me from doing that. The first, most practical reason being that we were outside, and therefore I had no door to close in their face even if I was so inclined. Secondly, I was curious. What message is so powerful that it compels these people to don church clothes on a hot August day and set out on foot to visit homes to which they are uninvited, petitioning people who don't want to see them, to deliver a message they don't want to hear? What makes the stakes so high for them? Are they driven by hope, by faith, by fear for me or for themselves? I was as surprised as they were to hear myself invite them onto the porch to have a seat. They had roughly fifteen minutes or so to tell me their story.

What followed was a standard pitch from which I could not sway them. There was an interesting moment, though, when the husband, after a few shared looks with his wife, nervously asked if I was Michael J. Fox. I confirmed the ID but had to ask how two followers of their particular faith would recognize me from television or the movies, when, as I understood it, those pastimes were forbidden. Having no answer for this, they shifted the conversation away from their transgression and back to the subject of my salvation. You could say that my willingness to hear them out was an expression of *my* faith, my instinct that it's always good to give something when I can. I like to think that I'm open to other people, unafraid of new ideas. It was unlikely that during those few minutes on the porch I could be coerced into surrendering my soul, so there was no reason why I couldn't surrender a few minutes of my time. This was an opportunity to hear their point of view, not defend my own. All I had to do was sit down and listen.

Listening to people espouse beliefs different from mine is informative, not threatening, because the only thing that can alter my worldview is a new and undeniable truth, and contrary to what Jack Nicholson says in *A Few Good Men,* "I *can* handle the truth."

A number of times over the next couple of weeks, I would return home from the gym, the tennis court, or the beach, and Tracy would tell me that *my friends* had been by again, or

I'd find telltale signs that they'd been there—fresh tracts on the porch.

By participating as I had in the midterm elections the previous fall, I had asked people to allow me onto their porch for a minute or two to hear what I had to say. I wore a jacket and a collared shirt, spoke politely, and was sincere in my promise to respect their point of view. Many allowed me the privilege. Some obviously saw me as a trespasser and let loose the attack dogs to growl, gnash their teeth, and bark loud enough to drown out my message, scare me away, or both. I was gratified and inspired that so many Americans did sit and listen to what I had to say, and found some truth in it.

If listening is an expression of optimism, it would seem that the results of the 2006 midterm election spoke to a rising tide of optimism in this country and perhaps our growing faith in one another. I've always considered faith to be an aspect or facet of optimism, a cousin of, if not a synonym for, hope. A discussion of faith as religion is a more daunting proposition. I haven't made and kept as many friends as I have by offering up my attitudes and opinions about religion. I am not a theologian, seminarian, or student of divinity. I have no argument with those who see in organized religion a template or an imperative to live life according to a prescribed set of beliefs. Just give others the room, within the laws of civil society, to believe or not believe whatever they like.

I've had many religious experiences over the years—good, bad, and ambivalent—with a number of dogmas and denominations, but never have I been a consistent and obedient disciple of any one big "F" Faith. At the risk of sounding New-Agey, I do consider myself a spiritual person. Too blessed to be strictly agnostic, I have come to adhere to an ethical code informed by the basic tenets of the major monotheistic disciplines: "Do unto others as you would have them do unto you," "Judge not lest ye yourself be judged," and at least a half dozen of the Commandments.

"The opposite of fear is faith" is an adage I heard often when I quit drinking. The thinking is that fear is paralyzing or even regressive, causing you to retreat in defense, while faith inspires forward progress. So why, I always wondered, does fear feature so prominently in our discussions and practice of faith? We talk about fear of God as a good thing—and being God-fearing as a desirable state. I know I'm not the first to say this, and smarter people have given it more thorough examination and more eloquent expression, but that just makes no sense to me. It's counterintuitive and, I think, confuses fear with respect. As a way of motivating people, cultivating fear is easier than investing the time and effort necessary to engender respect. Respect requires greater knowledge, and in my experience, the more you know, the less you fear.

In the year or so between my Parkinson's diagnosis and my quitting drinking, I had considered getting sober but feared life without the perceived buffer of alcohol. What I came to realize after a few months of disciplined sobriety was that my fear had nothing to do with alcohol or a lack thereof. It had to do with a lack of self-understanding. As I gained a more intimate knowledge of myself, why I did the things I did, what my resentments were, and how I could address them, my fear began to subside.

The same holds true for Parkinson's. I feared it most when I least understood it—the early days, months, and years after I was first diagnosed. It seems strange to say it, but I had to learn to respect Parkinson's disease. Instead of being reactive, I started being proactive, reading all the materials available, meeting with doctors, surgeons, researchers, and finally, after many years of lingering fear, getting to know fellow Parkinson's patients and other members of the community. Respecting it, however, doesn't mean tolerating it. And you can only vanquish an enemy you respect, have fully sized up, and weighed by every possible measure.

Understanding that Parkinson's is a neurological process, albeit a destructive one, depersonalized it and made it less sinister. In the same way, getting sober and being in the company of other people with the same issue, people whom I liked and held in high regard, made it clear that alcoholism was less a moral failing than a physical disease. So while my experiences with both alcohol and Parkinson's led me in many ways to a more spiritual way of looking at life, I didn't trade my fear of Parkinson's for a fear of God. Rather my respect for Parkinson's developed into a respect for a higher power.

When I was growing up, what baffled me about religion, particularly the hellfire and brimstone, Satan-centered variety, was that the devil seemed to get all the respect and God seemed to get all the fear. As a child in Vancouver, I couldn't wait for the last week in August when we'd go to the Pacific National Exhibition, our version of the state fair. There were of course the rides, the funnel cakes and cotton candy, the agricultural and trade exhibitions. Also scattered around the fairgrounds were attractions and presentations promoting various social and service groups, including religious organizations. When I was eight or nine, an evangelical church had parked a converted school bus, brightly painted in the style of the Partridge Family bus. Next to it, a playground had been set up with benches for parents to rest while their kids swung and teeter-tottered. Inevitably, most of the kids found their way up a few short stairs and into the bus, where a Bible lesson was continually in session. The vehicle's interior, absent its bench seats, had been outfitted with small chairs, the walls and windows papered with religiously themed art and instructional materials, so that it really did resemble a miniature classroom. As I climbed aboard, I immediately detected a sulfurous smell. A man at the far end of the vehicle crouched over a large bakelite ashtray. Speaking to the three or four kids already present, he lit a wooden kitchen match and tipped the head downward so the flame licked the matchstick. His other hand hovering a few inches above the tiny fire, he said, "I wouldn't want to get any closer to this because it would burn me. And that would hurt, right?"

The young audience nervously agreed.

"Now imagine thousands of these burning every part of your body, every inch of your skin. You would just be *screaming* in pain. Well, kids, that's what hell's like. And it lasts forever. But here's the good news . . ."

I didn't stick around for the good news.

Basically, the whole production just seemed silly to me. I had heard my parents, teachers, and hockey coaches make effective points, teach lessons, and instill values without having to scare the living crap out of me. My curiosity went more to why this grown man would devote time and energy to frightening kids with a box of matches. Why not just talk about how great heaven was? In retrospect, the answer is obvious. For a nine-year-old, heaven existed just outside of that Bible Bus—the distance of the few steps it took to reach the midway and the rides, noise, mystery, and mayhem of a summer day. Beyond the fair, there were a thousand further iterations of heaven—camping trips and hockey games, leaning forward in social studies class to get the full effect of whatever shampoo that pretty girl who sat in front of me was using. It never occurred to me that any of these pleasures were a reward for being a pretty good kid, any more than I needed to restructure my life just to avoid an eternity of being spit-roasted on a subterranean barbecue.

If this sounds flip, smug, or disrespectful, it's not meant to be. Obviously there is great wisdom, beauty, and relevance in millennia worth of collected theological teachings from around the world. The question I'm grappling with is: why didn't these big themes and major stick-and-carrot extremes resonate with me? I just never bought into the concept. Maybe I'm part of a small minority, but I don't think so.

One night last summer while watching TV, I saw a man who had, until very recently, lived his life in precisely that way—equating faith with fear. A powerful churchman with a congregation numbering in the thousands, Bishop Carlton D. Pearson described to an interviewer on ABC's 20/20 an epiphany that changed his life. It occurred while he himself was watching a news report on the terrible plight of Rwandan refugees. "I remember thinking that these were probably Muslims because God wouldn't let that happen to Christians," he said. "And that's when I said, 'God, how could you, how could you call yourself a loving God and a living God, and just let them suffer like that, and then to suck them into hell?' That's when I thought I heard an inner voice say, 'Can't you see they're already there?'"

He internalized these words as a message of love and inclusion and a refutation of judgment and condemnation. *There is no hell.*

Now, for me, watching in my living room, this was not "big news." I never saw life as a proving ground where you either earn enough points to spend forever in the clouds by the right hand of God or enough demerits to doom you to an eternity as an extra in a movie written by Dante and directed by Hieronymus Bosch. I never envisioned a God so bored that He'd have us scramble like rats through a Skinner box purely for His amusement.

But for Bishop Pearson, consider the personal, political, and spiritual ramifications of someone in his position, a no-nonsense soldier of God and saver of souls. The Devil had always featured prominently in his rhetoric and shaped his religious worldview. "I expected devils, I expected demons, I saw them everywhere, so that was part of my life," he told NPR's *This American Life*. "The Devil was as present and as large as God. He had most of the people and he was ultimately gonna get most of the people. Demons were all over in churches and schools, everything was the Devil. So if you believe it, you experience it."

I was riveted as he recounted to *20/20* the consequence of sharing his epiphany with his congregation at Higher Dimensions, part of the landscape of America's new mega-churches. The church hierarchy and the majority of the evangelical community in his hometown of Tulsa, Oklahoma, and throughout the country, condemned him for blasphemy. Their rhetoric and punishment had a scriptural quality to it. "The body of Christ at large should now ignore him. Don't support him, don't acknowledge him, don't attend his events, and don't dignify his position with time and attention. And, where necessary, protect the unaware from his teaching," decreed the president of the National Association of Evangelicals, Ted Haggard.

The same Ted Haggard, a fierce opponent of gay marriage, admitted in November of 2006 that he had received a massage from a Denver man, who himself claimed that a sex-for-pay arrangement had existed between the two men for over three years. Haggard also admitted that he bought methamphetamine through the man's connections. Haggard was forgiven by many of the same people that amen-ed his renunciation of Bishop Pearson. James Dobson, vocal spokesman for the Evangelical Christian movement and founder of the fundamentalist Focus on the Family, said this about Haggard: "He will continue to be my friend, even if the worst allegations prove accurate." Their pardons and prayers might save Haggard from hell, but Carlton Pearson would assert that Haggard had already been living in hell by way of his hypocrisy, homophobia, and humiliation.

Bishop Pearson, however, lost his church as well as the respect and support of the people he'd known, served, and worshipped with throughout his life. It wasn't just that it was a dizzying fall from grace; it was a *jump* from grace, or *into* grace.

For me, Haggard's warnings were reason enough: I had to meet Bishop Pearson. Superficially, there would seem to be no connection. We couldn't be two more different people. He's African-American; I'm whiter than Wonder Bread. He's an Evangelical living on "the buckle of the Bible Belt"; I'm a lapsed Protestant who attends a Reform Jewish synagogue in New York City. But in the same way I related to FDR's pronouncement that "the only thing we have to fear is fear itself," I was impressed by Bishop Pearson's courage in taking on fear. I can only read about FDR, but with a little effort and a couple of (I imagine unexpected) phone calls, I could actually arrange to meet the bishop.

TULSA, OKLAHOMA · DECEMBER 2007

After six and a half bumpy hours on two flights with a connection in Dallas, my writing assistant, Asher Spiller, and I are finally landing in Oklahoma, where it indeed feels as if the wind is sweeping down our plane. It's 7:00 P.M. Tulsa time, and having only carry-on luggage, we quickly locate our driver. She's a pleasant-looking woman holding a sign, the name on which I recognize as my nom de travel, a phony name she has no way of associating with the familiar face suddenly before her. We both seem to be wondering, What am I doing in Tulsa, Oklahoma?

On this leg of the journey, I suppose I could describe myself as sort of a reverse Dorothy, leaving the Oz of Manhattan, traveling through the storm to eventually thud down in the flat, monochromatic landscape of the American Plains. I'm not here to see the Wizard, more like someone who had the requisite opportunity and audacity to pull back the curtain.

At the Doubletree Inn we check in, ditch our bags in our rooms, and head down to the hotel's restaurant. The Warren Duck Club Grill, like what little we've seen of the rest of Tulsa in the hour we've been here, appears almost empty. Asher and I are led toward a round table at the far end of the dining room. Shaking my hand with a tight grip, Bishop Carlton D. Pearson pulls me into a hug. This gesture of familiarity doesn't seem strange given that we both, for obvious reasons, know each other better than do most people meeting for the first time.

A fit, fiftyish African-American, he's not tall, having maybe a couple of inches on me, but he cuts a striking figure. He's dressed entirely in black, and his shirt is open at the collar, his black horn-rimmed glasses are stylishly narrow and rectangular, and his impeccably groomed pencil mustache brackets the corners of his smile, with its ends meeting in a trim goatee. He is equal parts James Brown and Johnny Cash, in not only the physical sense, but also the spiritual—beyond appearance to experience, from "I Feel Good" to "Ring of Fire." As the next two or three hours pass, a conversation unfolds wherein the bishop shares a story I've come halfway across the country to hear firsthand.

Even knowing that Bishop Pearson is a veteran preacher, TV personality, and, in many ways, performer, it's still remarkable how readily and candidly he shares his story with me. After all, I am basically a stranger with a vaguely articulated agenda. I ask him about the formative effect of growing up in a household where both God and Satan were as alive and present as any member of the family. The way he tells it, in his family, you were either moving toward God and away from the Devil or vice versa, and if you lost track of where you stood presently, someone was always happy to remind you. This didn't just apply to the here and now, but to eternity as well.

He tells us that when he would ask his widowed aunt about how long it had been since her late husband, a backslider and incorrigible sinner, passed away, it was only natural to phrase the question, "Auntie, how long has Uncle T.D. been in hell?"

This aunt, whom Carlton describes as immensely God-fearing and churchly, not only accepted that her husband resided in hell, but also worried that in spite of her own piety, she was bound to join him there. To deny the existence of hell was not only a reversal of everything Carlton had believed in up to that point, but also an admission of his culpability in promoting a damaging myth to the countless thousands to whom he had ministered.

There is a wistfulness in the bishop's voice and a deep sense of loss. As he speaks, he pushes his napkin around the tabletop with his fingers. It's all a fitting prelude to what comes next—a guided tour of his lost kingdom.

Maybe I'm paranoid, but as we wait for the valet parking guy to bring the pastor's car around, a woman seated in the hotel lobby fixes me with a dark, thousand-yard stare, which she breaks only for a few seconds in order to offer the same to the bishop. It's surely my imagination, but it's really a case of "if you think it, you feel it," and it gives me a small appreciation for what it must be like to be the recipient of seething silent animus. As my host will remind me later, he may be the hometown heretic, but for my political views on stem cell research, I too am equally reviled by many in these parts—a slightly more exotic but still-dangerous infidel.

I ride shotgun as we pull out of the parking lot and into light traffic. Dominating the skyline in Tulsa is the eighty-eight-story CityPlex Towers. Originally christened "The City of Faith," the skyscraper was commissioned in the late seventies by Oral Roberts, pioneering giant of Christian broadcasting. He meant to make Tulsa the center of God's enterprise on earth and, in fact, the skyscraper had been built according to the instructions of a nine-hundred-foot-tall Jesus that appeared to Roberts in a dream. Jesus' specs called for the construction to be at least a foot taller than the BOK Tower, at that time the highest point on the Tulsa skyscape. Visitors to the city find it a useful navigational reference, and as we are particularly interested in exploring the impact Oral Roberts's ministry has had on this city and its people, the towers serve as a North Star to the Roberts constellation of holdings and properties. The bishop's ties to the aging evangelist and his empire are deep and complex, although, in spite of his time and service, his conversion to inclusive theology has found him effectively excommunicated from the Oral Roberts ministry.

The wider evangelical world, I know, is made up of dozens of individual fiefdoms, large and small. As an expert on the intrigues and heraldry of the various charismatic communities, the bishop peppers his dialogue with references to famous preachers and proselytizers. At dinner the night before, during breakfast, and now here in the car, he expresses surprise at my familiarity with such Evangelical personalities as Benny Hinn, Paul and Jan Crouch, and Carman, a sort of gospel Tom Jones. Frankly, it freaks me out too.

Rex Humbard, Kathryn Kuhlman, Oral Roberts, Billy Graham, Ernest Angley, Jerry Falwell, Jim and Tammy—I realize that this moment with Bishop Carlton D. Pearson is a logical extension of a lifelong fascination with preachers and preaching. I think that early on in my life there was some seeking of divine affirmation. But I understand by now that, really, I just dug the showbiz, the flamboyant theatricality, and all that rich, unintended irony.

When channel surfing on DirectTV, I unconsciously slow down as I pass through channels 372 to 379. This is what I call Gospel Gulch, a series of satellite stations expressly dedicated to evangelical outreach. The next thumb-flick could reveal anything from an earnest soloist performing an achingly beautiful version of some hymn you half-remember from childhood, to *Wrestlers for Jesus* entertaining a gymnasium full of teenagers by slamming each other with folding chairs in the name of the Lord.

Not too long ago I devoted an entire insomniac hour to a panel show featuring born-again stand-up comedians, each taking turns doing five-minute sets. They seemed to be of two schools: the always-been-religious guy, clown of his Sunday Bible class, firing off knee-slapper punch lines like "No, Barabbas, I *can't* see your house from here!"; and then there were the three or four funny guys who had lived hard secular lives, for whom coming to Jesus was not natural and maybe not even voluntary. Painfully familiar with both sides of the edge, they knew just where it lay and how close to it they could bring these church folk. An example of the old equation, "pain + time = comedy," their humor ventured into dark territory like their own battles with drug and alcohol addiction, provoking fear-based laughter. The audience's fear, I sensed, was not a reaction to the perils of a life of sin, but more a fear of the part of themselves that says, "That sounds like fun!"

As a beer-drinking teenager, I loved that my bedroom was in the basement, allowing me to slide in undetected at all hours. On many a Saturday night I fell asleep (or passed out) with my little rabbit-eared, black-and-white television still blaring. There were Sunday mornings when I'd wake from dreams rife with explicit religious themes and imagery— dreams about Jesus or dreams about traveling to Africa and distributing Bibles to poor villagers. I'd hear hymns in my dreams and people praying and speaking in tongues. It took a while for the teenage fog to lift enough for me to realize that no matter what they aired on that particular TV station at 2:30 A.M., by 8:00 A.M. they were showing *The 700 Club*. I was osmotically incorporating words and images from the television show into whatever unconscious adolescent psycho-stew was already brewing.

Growing up, I tended to have several clusters of friends, each group existing in a separate social orbit. In seventh grade, I made friends with a kid named Russell. He played drums, and I played the guitar. Our pre–White Stripes duo was the first "band" I played in throughout my youth. Strict and devoted Baptists, Russ's parents, two sisters, and brother welcomed me like family into their home and, as it was a natural extension, their church. Meals at their house meant enthusiastic and sincere grace-saying, long trips in their car meant singing rounds of religious spirituals, and hanging out on weekdays in the summer often meant going to church-sponsored youth camps. Not that I minded any of this. It was all kind of happy and uplifting. And whether it was a measure of their particular brand of faith or just an exception in my case, the hellfire and brimstone was kept to a minimum. There was an elegant and poignant beauty in their dedication to God. One spring vacation I traveled with Russ to his grandparents' farm deep in the interior of British Columbia. In the still-dark early Sunday morning, a family caravan on foot and ATV made its way to one of the taller hilltops on the property, raised a hand-hewn wooden cross, and performed Easter service as the sun rose.

But there was plenty of time to just be kids too. Russ had a spectacular tree house in his backyard, a two-minute bike ride from the apartment complex that I grew up in. And apparently there was no religious conflict for Russ when I brought over a *Playboy* magazine from which we tore photos to pin up on the walls. In the tree house we had a third partner in crime, a kid I'll call Lawrence. As far as I knew, Lawrence didn't take an interest or any part in the church side of Russell's life. He was a funny but moody kid. A lot of laughs when things were crazy, but when, for example, it came time to clean up or fix the roof or some other fort-related responsibility, Lawrence would strategically pick a fight and resign from the clubhouse. We'd just shrug.

The three of us had already started to drift apart in the eighth grade, when we heard the tragic news one Monday morning that after a weekend fight with his parents stemming from their refusal to let him attend a rock concert, Lawrence had gone up to his room, slung a belt over the edge of his closet door, and hanged himself. I wasn't sophisticated enough at the time to recognize it as such, but the tragedy pretty much marked the end of my childhood.

There was another brief round of churchgoing with Russ and his family, but not much of what I was hearing in sermons or at youth group seemed especially relevant to me. I had no anger, resentment, or sense of disillusionment about religion. I still thought the world of Russ and his family—it was just time to move on.

Russ grew up true to his faith. Still playing music, he became something of a singing missionary, performing gospel and folk-rock in churches across Canada. He married a woman with a passion for Jesus equal to his own, raised beautiful children, and, loading them all into a Winnebago, spent a couple of years traversing the continent. It was an incredible testament to his devotion, and his own imperative to witness, that he and his family endured the hardships of their vagabond lifestyle—home schooling, a lack of privacy, and not always welcoming audiences.

Out of respect for his commitment as well as a nostalgic gratitude for the kindness and love his family had shown me over the years, when Russ called me one day to solicit support for his missionary work, I was open and receptive. I sent him a check, although I specified that I would write it in his name and not that of his ministry. I wouldn't fund a church whose policies and practices I wasn't familiar with, but I felt comfortable helping Russ and his family do whatever it was that made them happy. A few years later, I helped him out again when he, his family, and a group of their friends were off to do relief work in Rwanda after the devastating tribal warfare there. And when Russ and his brother passed through New York, I let them crash on the foldout couch in my office. I haven't spoken to Russ about this directly, but it troubled me when shortly after I began to involve myself in the campaign for expanded stem cell research, he sent a letter telling me the good news that I would one day be cured of Parkinson's disease, but, he cautioned, it would be by purely supernatural means, not scientific. In other words, I should quit politicking and commence praying. He reminded me that during a New Year's party, 1972 into 1973, in our friend Rusty's basement, I had accepted Christ as my personal savior. Myself, I was a little fuzzy on those details. I remembered that I had a deep and spiritual interest in Rusty's rapidly developing big sister Karen, a born-again herself and a major player in the crusade to win eighth-grade souls for Christ. Anyway, it seemed to have had more of an impression on Russ over the years than it did on me. I put my checkbook away.

When I tell Bishop Pearson this story in Tulsa, his listening is punctuated by the occasional nod, but when I mention Russ's admonition about relying on God over science, the nod grows deeper and is lit by a knowing smile.

"You have to understand where your friend Russ is coming from. He's been praying for you and ministering to you for a long time, and with everything in his heart and soul, he believes that what he's saying is righteous." The light in the pastor's eye changes slightly and what follows is clearly his own take on what it would mean for the person who could convince me to renounce my position and embrace an Evangelical Christian point of view. "For you to say you were wrong, that you realize now that stem cells was just killin' babies, and that you know that Jesus alone can cure the sicknesses of the world, that would be huge."

I'm not ascribing those motives to Russ, although this is Carlton's world, and he knows it intimately, the showbiz side of it as well as the spiritual. Clearly Carlton feels a connection to this former life and the wider audience he once commanded. I've gained an even greater sense of what he sacrificed in laying bare the truth as he saw it. Even now, he keeps an office in a downtown Tulsa building, replete with ornate and overstuffed furniture, obviously part of a larger collection left over from his halcyon days at Higher Dimensions. He can't come up with a good explanation for why he hasn't left Tulsa yet and consistently uses words like "we" and "ours" when discussing the church and the community, including but not restricted to Oral Roberts and his ministry, who have dismissed him so completely.

It's not just a matter of one door closing and another opening. Carlton Pearson sees all doors as open, with the entirety of his experience available to him, and through his ministry, to others. This is the most obvious parallel I can draw between my experience and Carlton's. I had no idea what the future would hold for me once I stepped out of the comfort zone of my television career. I certainly didn't envision myself creating a foundation that would have such an impact on not only my life, but the lives of countless people I will probably never meet. What led me to that choice may have been God or may have just been an emerging practical need to do something positive. The purpose that you wish to find in life, like a cure you seek, is not going to fall from the sky. I think that Carlton is going through a similar process. It requires the faith to take risks and a rejection of the bonds of fear. I believe purpose is something for which one is responsible; it's not just divinely assigned.

As my time with the pastor—twenty-four hours spent over two days—is winding down, I try to pinpoint what exactly I'll be taking away from this place. I'm glad I came here. My experience in Tulsa has shown me that in some ways, the world is as simple as I sometimes see it and often wish it to be. In other ways, it is complicated beyond any understanding.

My conversations with Carlton have picked locks, reopening long-sealed memories of religious feelings and experiences. Over the course of my life, countless times I have, wittingly or not, positioned myself for spiritual rebirth. It's possible that on some level, that was my purpose here, but I don't think so. Neither was I on a mission to debunk anything. It's far more complicated than that. And infinitely more simple. The bishop, for all his eloquence on the subject of witnessing and the divine burden of winning souls for Christ, never made a pitch for mine. I think our connection had less to do with faith than a basic sense of optimism that led us down the paths we had chosen and grew stronger with time and distance traveled.

When I first exhibited the symptoms of PD, I was twenty-nine years old and living life, as I've described before, in an insular bubble. Space within the bubble would increase with every success and contract with every failure. But at the time, I had been on an amazing run professionally as well as personally, with my recent marriage and the birth of our son, Sam. So the bubble was plenty big. As it expanded, of course, the membrane grew thinner, tauter. I was afraid of what would happen if and when it finally ruptured. An explosion represented the worst-case scenario; a slow leak represented the best. My mistake was in thinking they were mutually exclusive.

In 1991, I learned the truth about the barely perceptible tics and tremors and aches and pains I had been experiencing over the course of the previous year, that they weren't the physical graffiti of hedonistic excess or athletic misadventure, but the symptoms of a progressively debilitating disease for which there was no cause and, even worse, no known cure. My world as I knew it had changed in the instant the doctor pronounced my condition. As an actor, I am used to processing other people's opinions of me—auditioners, audiences, and critics. You can take an opinion, rationalize it, and turn it back on those who offer it up as being their projections onto your reality. But it's rare that someone can present you with some great immutable truth about yourself—something so surprising, out of left field, that you don't even have the luxury of denial.

We do so much to protect ourselves from the truth, but what I have learned and drawn strength and comfort from, especially over the last seventeen years or so, is that the truth protects us from ourselves. That is, of course, if we can recognize it and trust it. As an epigraph before the first page of *Lucky Man,* I included a quote from Henry David Thoreau that I found particularly apt: "In accumulating property for ourselves or our posterity, in founding a family or a state, or acquiring fame even, we are mortal; but in dealing with truth we are immortal, and need fear no change nor accident."

What I'm saying is not that the great truth was Parkinson's specifically, but that there are realities that occur in life over which I have no control or influence, realities that I can't negotiate, finesse, or charm.

You could argue that the bishop's truth was subjective interpretation and mine was based on scientific fact. But there is no questioning his certainty, and just as I had to make adjustments and take actions that this new truth demanded of me, so did he. That first night, over the Oklahoma version of *antipasti,* Carlton commented on my courage in dealing with Parkinson's and my commitment to advocacy.

"The difference is," I explained, "I didn't choose to have Parkinson's. I agree that if I took on the condition and everything that comes with it just to be an advocate on behalf of others so afflicted, well then yeah, that would be historically heroic. But in a way, I am just rolling with the punches. *You* took this on. You could have kept your doubts and concerns to yourself and carried on doing what you had been doing, but you walked into this with your eyes wide open."

Maybe on that first day when he stood before his congregation and refuted the existence of hell, he didn't quite anticipate the reaction and the fallout. I believe him, though, when he says that he didn't have any choice but to tell the truth as he saw it, and that it might be the most important thing he'd ever do. And I believe him when he says that he has no second thoughts, in spite of the hardship and heartache it has brought to him and his family. Sure, here in his office, narrowed by the vestiges of a forfeited empire, he still looks a little shell-shocked. I know the feeling.

Whether you wield the pin yourself, as the bishop did, or the bubble is popped for you, the truth flows outside of it, and it will take you places you'd otherwise drift past.

Tikkun Olam

Our son, Sam, was born at Cedars Sinai Hospital in Los Angeles on May 30, 1989. He was enormous. And so, for both him and Tracy, labor and delivery had been strenuous and exhausting, although thankfully not too dramatic. We were allowed to keep him in the room with us for the roughly twenty-four hours we remained in the hospital. Nobody got much rest. Our son, it turned out, was a screamer. He spent those first few hours settling on the one or two shrill keening notes that would be his exclusive form of communication for the next six colicky months.

Understandably, Tracy wanted sleep. I was just trying to be helpful, although a twenty-seven-year-old first-time father is generally useless in this situation. Serving as a middleman between Tracy and the hospital administration, I consulted with the nurses about baby wrangling, and fielded phone calls from family and friends who wanted to know how Tracy was, how the baby was, when we were coming home, when they could visit, and above all, what we were going to name him. Somewhere in Tracy's overnight bag with the Lamaze book and the banana chips was a list of names we had been compiling and amending for weeks. There were some late-eighties-era classics (too embarrassing to repeat), but the name "Sam" was nowhere on our list. We agreed to wait twelve hours before deciding on a name. After ushering everyone out of the room, Tracy and I carefully considered this wriggling lump of child with the enormous hands and feet that lay before us.

"He looks like a truck driver," Tracy said.

"Yeah, like a teamster captain I know—Sam."

"Sam, that's good," she said.

It seemed so easy. *Is this how it works?* I wondered. Is this how your parents came up with the moniker you were stuck with for the rest of your life?

"Oh wait," Tracy said. "Sam Fox?"

"Yeah, Sam Fox," I said. I was ready to commit.

All of a sudden Tracy started to laugh uncontrollably. "Sam Fox?" she said, still giggling. "It's just so . . . so *Jewish*."

"Now I love it," I said.

Tracy is from a Jewish family, and though I hadn't converted, we were married under a *chuppah*. Over the ten years between my arrival in Los Angeles in 1979 and this moment in the hospital with my bride and newborn son, I had become happily immersed in the community and culture of American Reform Judaism. My friends, my associates, and now my family were for the most part Jews. My surname "Fox," common in the Lancastershire area from which my Church of England grandfather emigrated to Canada at the turn of the century, I also understood, was a common "Ellis Islandization" of a number of surnames common among Ashkenazi Jews of Eastern Europe. The name Sam Fox appealed to me because, while I wasn't Jewish, my son, borne by a Jewish mother, was, by definition and birthright. So it worked on a couple of levels.

Sam, of course, was oblivious to all this—his name, his religion, the size of his hands and feet. However, he would soon be painfully aware of the relevance of all of this, as it related to the immediate disposition of an entirely different appendage. The doctor visited our room to discuss circumcision. She was Jewish, and while she expressed her respect for whatever feelings we had on the procedure, there was no mistaking her advocacy. Tracy had qualms, if not deep misgivings, having nothing to do with religion or Judaism. While her family wasn't particularly observant, she certainly had no reservations about identifying as a Jew. But as a progressive, enlightened, American woman, raised in the seventies, she had a reflexive aversion to submitting her son to what could be described as ritual mutilation. To me, it was very clear, and I surprised myself by calmly and clearly making my point.

"I understand what you're saying, honey, and I'm not saying we have to do a *bris* and the whole floor show. But you're Jewish, so he's Jewish. He's part of a culture and a continuum that I can't even pretend to understand or fully appreciate. So let me put it this way: If the doctor does it now, here in the hospital, I'll go in the room with the two of them, and I'll hold him. And when she gets busy with the scalpel, I'll look him in the eye and give him someone to scream at. But in thirteen years, if he decides he wants to have a *bar mitzvah* and he isn't circumcised, then *you* are going to be in that room with him. I'm going to Vegas."

Now, I understand that people have strong opinions about this, but in my first major decision as a father, I felt it was right to connect Sam to a long cultural tradition outside of my own. So I cradled my son with a pre-PD steadiness and cooed at him while the doc did the deed. No doubt, it hurt him a hell of a lot more than it hurt me. Thirteen years later, my mother, brother, and sisters, Anglo-Irish Protestants from the west coast of Canada, flew to New York and sat in a synagogue for the first time in their lives and watched proudly as Sam was welcomed into the adult world.

It was Sam who came to us at age nine and asked us to send him to Hebrew school. He had learned from his friends at school that he'd have to start religious training now if he wanted to be *bar mitzvahed* in four years' time. Naturally, Tracy was more savvy about all this than I was, and after several inquiries into New York synagogues, she liked what she heard about Central. Having never been to the synagogue itself, we joined that summer with plans to start attending when we returned from vacation in the fall.

On Friday afternoon, August 28, I flipped on the television at our summer rental on Long Island, and the first image that appeared on the screen was helicopter footage of a horrific inferno in what looked to be midtown Manhattan. It was hard to hear the report clearly over the whir of the chopper blades, but two words did stand out clearly: *Central Synagogue.*

"Tracy," I called into the kitchen where she was helping the girls to a snack. "What was the name of that synagogue we just joined?"

"Central," she replied.

"I think it just burned down."

The building had been undergoing renovation, and the fire was caused by a blowtorch used by workmen installing a new air-conditioning system. Luckily no one was hurt, but from what I'd been able to learn from news reports and my own research, the loss was tremendous. Built in 1872, the building was a registered landmark and widely considered one of the most beautiful houses of worship in the world. Although it would take a massive effort and untold millions of dollars, Rabbi Peter Rubinstein promised the shocked and sobbing congregants who gathered the next morning to witness the damage that they would rebuild. "We have work to do, and we shall do it."

There is a Hebrew expression, actually the way I understand it, it's more of a principle of Judaism—*tikkun olam* (tuhk-OON-oh-LAH-m), which translates into English as "repairing the world." This was first explained to me by Rabbi Josh Davidson, the young protégé of Rabbi Rubinstein, who helped prepare Sam for his *bar mitzvah.*

The conversation took place in early September of 2001. It was an exciting time for the Central Synagogue community. The lengthy repairs after the fire were near completion and the sanctuary was about to reopen. Sam was one of the small army of kids set to work with paints and brushes, adding finishing touches to the ornate stencil work that graced nearly every wall and corner of the building's interior. Rabbi Rubinstein of course would conduct services celebrating the building's reopening, but Rabbi Davidson was preparing a service for the following week. He wanted to talk about stem cells, and he called me for some background information. I was prepared to be put on the defensive. At a time when the profile of this new research was still emerging, it seemed that whenever a religious authority weighed in, his or her position was starkly negative. Josh was pleasant, though, and his questions came from a place of honest curiosity and empathy for those whose lives might be improved or saved. Jewish tradition, he explained, has always encouraged scientific and medical advances. In that context, stem cell research, far from being destructive or evil, is an embodiment of the *mitzvah* of healing. We all have a responsibility to do what we can for those living among us, those we love and those we've never met. This was when I first heard about *tikkun olam*.

Josh assured me that whatever my endeavors in this arena, he and the synagogue were fully behind me. I thanked him, and I said I looked forward to being in the congregation and hearing what he had to say on the subject. Between the phone call and the sermon fell Tuesday, September 11, 2001. The notion of repairing the world took on a more urgent and dramatic dimension. Rabbi Davidson put aside his stem cell sermon for a while.

Among the speakers scheduled to toast Sam at his *bar mitzvah* celebration were my brother—Sam's uncle Steve—and Tracy's brother, Michael. Not on the roster—me. I was cool with that. On plenty of occasions leading up to the *bar mitzvah* I had told Sam how proud I was of him, so when he specifically requested that I not make a speech, I was happy to be relieved of the responsibility, without feeling deprived of an opportunity. Unbeknownst to me, at least until we arrived at the rented hall, Sam had a change of heart and decided he would like me to say a few words. I had none prepared, and even if I did, there was now a whole drug-timing issue to deal with. The acidy taste of panic rising in my throat, I pulled Tracy aside. Turns out Sam had approached her first, hoping she would ask me to speak.

"He'll do it, honey," she assured him, "but you have to ask him yourself."

I complimented her on the well-taught lesson at my expense.

"Just tell a 'Sam story,'" she said. "Tell the bike story."

Sam was never a "play catch with the old man in the backyard" kind of kid. Any attempt on my part in the first six or seven years of his life to interest him in sports-related activities, including the ones I played as a kid, like hockey, baseball, and basketball, was politely but firmly rebuffed. Sam had his own reasons for this, and some of them actually made a lot of sense. When he was six, I took him down to the field house at Chelsea Piers with the intention of registering him for the boys' soccer program. We met up with a super-eager young volunteer coach, who explained to us that there were two kinds of programs: one that focused on fundamentals with very little direct competition between teams, and then, of course, the real thing—a competitive league with games scheduled between established teams. It had been obvious to me from the outset that Sam really didn't want to do either. But he was a sweet kid, so perhaps he'd humor me.

After a brief pause in which I could have inserted a silent "If I really have to," he said he'd pick the instructional league.

I was a little disappointed, but I tried not to let it show. "That's great, Sam, but what's wrong with the competitive league? Don't you want to play against real teams in a real league?"

He shook his head. "Nah," he said. "Too much arguing."

He had a point, and, getting a clear sense that he wasn't too hot on the instructional league either, I didn't push. We left without registering for either. After all, it wasn't that he was a sedentary kid. He loved running around, roughhousing, trampling through the woods with me on bug hunts, and he had learned to swim at an early age in any sizeable body of available water—a pool, a pond, or an ocean. Still, he didn't seem to have a tremendous amount of self-confidence in the area of athletic activities.

Having grown up playing a variety of youth sports, I had experienced my share of pushy parents, projecting their own unfulfilled ambitions to become superjocks on their children, who could never play hard enough or be good enough to win enough. Sam didn't want to play sports, and Tracy and I decided that was cool with us.

There was, however, one caveat. When, by the age of seven, he had still refused to learn how to ride a bicycle, I put my foot down. I told Tracy that I had to teach him. That's what dads are supposed to do. It's like a law or something. I think they take away your dad license if you break it. No matter how much he resisted, I had decided to be patient but persistent. That summer, I formulated a plan to use the two-week period we'd be spending at our farm in Vermont to get Sam up on two wheels.

Sam's aversion to any form of auto-locomotion other than walking, running, and swimming, as well as his refusal to ride anything other than my shoulders or the occasional rented pony, was all-encompassing to the point where he'd never even embraced the technology of a tricycle—never mind training wheels. "All the better," I decided. "Let's just get straight down to business."

At the top of our driveway leading to the barn, the ground flattened out into a gravel area sizeable enough for a kid on a bike to pick up some steam and carry on for a reasonable distance. I approached the helmeted Sam, sitting on the bike's saddle, and gripped the back of the seat with my right hand and the handle bar with my left. Once completely upright, he began a steady roll forward. As soon as I was jogging at a speed great enough to create equilibrium, I asked Sam if I could let go. The scream that he offered as a reply was frantic, forceful, and completely unintelligible, but I understood the gist of it: "NO FUCKING WAY!"

The problem, Sam explained to me later through tears of frustration, was that the gravel was too loose and scrambly, and he had felt like the bike was going to slip out sideways from underneath him at any moment. I thought his analysis was a positive step and implied a desire for forward progress.

"You know what we could do?" I said. "The parking lot down at the volunteer fire hall is always empty, and it has that smooth, paved surface with no hills. Why don't we throw the bike in the back of the truck and head down there?"

"Okay," Sam said. But as he spoke the words, the rest of his face made it clear that he had *anything* else to do.

After only a few minutes of going through the motions down by the South Woodstock Fire Hall, it became obvious that the new conditions were no better. While the surface was certainly smoother, it was also harder, and the prospect of falling down or flying over the handlebars was all the more terrifying to Sam. I decided that somehow, somewhere, we'd eventually find the perfect classroom to provide the tutorial. But this wasn't working. I felt bad for Sam. I felt bad for me.

Perhaps sensing an opportunity to put an end to this charade, at least for the day, and maybe make both of us feel a little bit better, Sam had a suggestion: "Why don't we go get some ice cream?"

"Sounds good to me," I said.

After I returned the bike to the back of the pickup truck and strapped Sam to his booster seat in the crew cab, we crossed over a covered bridge, took a left on Route 4, and soon arrived at a soft-serve joint that (except for the prices) was right out of the fifties.

Sitting on a sticky picnic table, Sam sucked the entire double shot of chocolate swirl through the hole he had bitten in the bottom of his cone while I poked at the ice chunks in my frappe with a straw. Neither of us even mentioned the word "bicycle," and after fifteen minutes or so, we were back in the truck, heading home. On our way to the covered bridge, we passed the high school, or more accurately, its playing fields, including the freshly mowed but completely empty baseball diamond. Before I even had a complete understanding of why, I found myself pulling off the highway, proceeding to the far end of the faculty parking lot, and stopping behind the chain-linked backstop. The plan was finally formed by the time I had Sam on the bike at home plate, his front wheel pointed at first base. The base paths, to paraphrase the fairy tale, were "just right"—solid enough to prevent any shimmying of the wheels, but soft enough that should my seven-year-old son be dislodged from his Schwinn, he probably wouldn't suffer so much as a knee scrape. Sam was finding a comfort level, and after a few dry runs from home to first with me holding the bike, he was ready to try at least part of it solo.

"Okay," I said, "I'll get you started and then run ahead of you to the base and catch you when you get there."

It amazed me how quickly he was able to accomplish what just that morning had seemed impossible. And it was relatively easy to convince him to make the turn from first to second, where I would gently halt his forward progress just as I had done at first. Fifteen minutes later, he was ready to do a triple-bagger and then on to home. Within forty-five minutes of arriving at the ball field, I was sitting on the pitcher's mound, loudly sucking the warm, melted remains of my shake through my chewed-up flexi-straw, while Sam, the Babe Ruth of bicycling, pedaled out home run after home run.

Confident that this could carry on without more input from me, I sauntered toward the garbage can on the other side of the fence that bordered the third-to-home base path. When I turned back after disposing of my cup, I expected to feel the ever-so-slight displacement of air created by a seven-year-old rolling by on his bike. But Sam wasn't, as far as I could tell, anywhere on the base paths. The scope of my search widened, and then I saw him. As he set out on this latest revolution, for reasons known only to him, he felt emboldened to skip the left at first and pedal straight into the outfield. Maneuvering a bike through the grass is more challenging, but with his legs pumping like pistons, he made steady if increasingly serpentine progress. It suddenly occurred to me that, as much as I had managed to teach him about riding a bike, the one lesson I hadn't given yet was how to stop. Breaking into a sprint, I hoped to reach him before he grew panicked by the same realization. I was close, about five feet behind him, when it happened. Perhaps he hit a bump, his foot slipped off the pedal, or he just lost his concentration, but down he went in a clattering heap. Pulling him to his feet for a quick once-over, I was surprised to see that he wasn't crying. In fact, he was grinning like a chimp. He was even a little impatient. "Put me back on the bike, Dad, and give me a push," he said. I did. And he was gone. Every once in a while, he would slow down just enough to let me catch up, but he was no longer following the careful geometry of my plan. He was finding his own path.

That's the story I told at Sam's *bar mitzvah*. As I looked out at the faces of friends and family around the room, I knew I didn't have to stall the dessert course any longer by breaking down the symbolism.

Obviously a big deal for Sam, what I found surprising was what a profound impact his *bar mitzvah* had on me. My adolescent experience featured no equivalent ritual, a formal merging of childhood with adult responsibility. This may be putting it rather harshly, but for me and the friends I grew up with, thirteen was not an age at which anyone threw us a big party welcoming us into the world of grown-ups. Spotty, smelly, increasingly hairy, unsure of our words, and awkward in our movements, we responded to cues, some tacit, some explicit, that now was the time to play defense. Just slither away and get through it; get through high school; if you're lucky, get a job; and if you're real lucky, get a union job.

The Jewish culture, as I was beginning to understand it, places structure and ritual around this transition, instructing these emerging life forms to recognize and accept their responsibility to themselves, their families, and others. They are claimed and celebrated just when they are most susceptible to feeling unwanted and misunderstood.

Personally, I couldn't even get that right, at least not in that order. A few months before my eighteenth birthday, already a high school dropout, with my father as a dubious but dutiful chauffeur, I went south from Vancouver to California to find an agent and pursue a career. It wasn't quite a *bar mitzvah*, but that long drive down Interstate 5 was as close as I came to experiencing a definitive coming-of-age ritual.

Eager and forward-looking, not yet having developed that tiny region of brain matter designed to identify and avoid risk, I didn't see this as much as a rejection of the past as I saw it as an embrace of the future. But it's ironic that I definitely needed the guidance of an adult, at least this one last time, not to bring me into a community but to deliver me from one. Not knowing what the heck it was that I was looking for, my father, at the very least, knew that I wasn't likely to find it at home.

I don't know if I fully realized it at first, but a lot of the ac-quaintances I made upon arriving in Los Angeles and insinu-ating myself into the entertainment industry were Jewish people—my agents, my managers, and many of the directors, producers, and actors I worked with, as well. It seems so funny now, but at barely eighteen years old, fresh from west-ern Canada with its largely working class Anglo-Saxon popu-lation, albeit with sizeable representations from Hong Kong and India (former British colonies), any concept I had of Juda-ism was based on the Old Testament and the self-deprecating jokes comics made on *The Tonight Show*. Maybe a year later I started to put it together: *I'm the only guy with plans for the twenty-fifth of December.*

Families took me in for meals and family celebrations, and theirs was a warmth and humor that I related to. This had little to do with religion as I experienced it. I couldn't speak for the spiritual lives of my new friends, but for me, it had ev-erything to do with culture. My experience with Russ and his family, whose culture and religion (though more fervent) were essentially my own, seemed much more exotic to me than the Jewish culture in which I was quickly beginning to feel at home.

The producer/director Garry Marshall gave me his theory regarding my success in comedy: "You've got Jewish timing," he said, "and a *goyishe punim.*" That is to say, I can deliver a joke in a style that has its roots in Yiddish theater, but I look like the typical "boy next door." Alex Keaton, a Waspy Midwestern lad of the eighties, was largely the creation of a group of Jewish comedy writers led by Gary Goldberg, a product of a Jewish neighborhood in Brooklyn. The rhythms of the patter, the emphasis on percussive consonants like Ps and Ks, answering questions with inverted responses that in themselves are questions, like "Upset? Why would I be upset?"—these are all characteristics of television comedy that are rooted in the traditions of Jewish humor. This comedy and the comedians who introduced it to me via television, from Phil Silvers to Milton Berle, to Mel Brooks, to Jerry Seinfeld, were, for the most part, Jewish, and their experiences informed my own, whether I realized it or not. My affinity for this tradition of Jewish comedic expression was just the professional iteration of a larger connection that I have found myself making in all areas of my life.

In 1985, in an interview with *People* magazine, I was asked if I planned to marry one day. "Oh yes, definitely," I said. "I'm going to marry a Jewish girl." When the reporter asked me why, I said something along the lines of "Because I won't have to make any decisions, and I can eat Chinese food on Sundays." I was half-right—sometimes we have Indian.

It's fair to say that I have staked a claim in Judaism. I've married a Jewish girl, and we are raising our children in the Jewish culture and, moreover, in the Jewish faith—our three oldest have been *bar* and *bat mitzvahed*. Last February, on the Thursday before Aquinnah and Schuyler were to be called to the *bema*, Tracy and I brought the girls to the synagogue for a run-through of the proceedings and a chance to read through the sermons each of them had prepared based on their Torah portions.

Rabbi Peter Rubinstein is a compact, energetic man in his fifties who could be a double for Duke basketball coach Mike Krzyzewski. In addition to their striking physical resemblance, Rabbi Rubinstein and Coach K share a dynamic approach to leadership and have earned much loyalty and respect. The rabbi walked us through what was required of each of us—candles to light, prayers to read in Hebrew and, luckily for me, in English. He showed us how to handle the Torah as we passed it family member to family member, generation to generation. Notes were given to the girls on their readings, mostly praise, with gentle reminders to look up every now and then to make eye contact with the congregation. Most compelling and resonant about that evening, though, were the words he shared just before we left the sanctuary. He reminded the girls that they were becoming part of an incredible lineage, a tradition that had endured centuries of oppression and persecution. I felt a mixture of both pride and humility over my role in bringing them to this place. Evident in their faces was the realization that much of what was good in their lives—family, freedom, security—was connected to a long history of struggle, and their public declaration of belonging had once brought a heavy price.

At the same time, I had no countervailing feeling that by sanctioning this identification by my children with their mother's religion and culture, I was rejecting my own. As for religious traditions, I really had none. I was nominally an Anglican, in that my mom, dad, and their families were members of and (some more than others) attended the Church of England. When I was growing up, however, other than Sunday school at the church on our military base, and the occasional Christmas or Easter service, we weren't church people.

Culturally—now, this is where it gets interesting to me—our customs and traditions, while different from Judaism in many ways, seemed to be informed by a similar ethic. These were good people, my family, my friends. They honored fairness, fidelity, honesty, family, and hard work. They made sacrifices for their countries in war and peace. They were far more gratified for what they had than bitter for what they did not, and I related to how the religious tradition of Tracy and her family was inclusive and accepting and placed a great emphasis on spiritual and intellectual curiosity.

One of my nephews, Isaac, seven years old at the time, once hit me with this out-of-the-blue question: "I don't get it, are you Jewish or are you Christmas?"

My own son, Sam, at an even younger age, returned from preschool one day with a tin of cookies he and his classmates had baked that day—golden, buttery, tricornered shortbread efforts with a dollop of fruit in the center. He told me they were *Hamantashen* cookies for Purim.

"*Haman . . . tashen?*" I asked.

"Yeah," he replied. "They're shaped like this bad guy named Haman's hat . . . for Purim . . . you know?"

"Actually," I had to admit, "no, I don't."

"Oh, that's right," he almost apologetically remembered. "You're not a Jew."

When I recall exchanges like these, I'm reminded that my world is so thoroughly immersed in Jewish culture and tradition that even those closest to me often forget that I was not born into it.

CENTRAL SYNAGOGUE, NEW YORK CITY
SEPTEMBER 2007

In September of 2007, as I was shepherding my family into the sanctuary of Central Synagogue for the Rosh Hashanah service, Rabbi Rubinstein stood near the foot of the *bema*, conversing with a cluster of congregants. Noticing me, he gave a quick friendly wave and began to make his way over. Tracy and the kids were just filing past me and were taking the last few seats in the fourth pew when Rabbi Rubinstein approached, greeting me with a warm hug and a welcoming smile.

"I refer to you in the sermon today," he informed me. "Not by name, of course," he assured me. "It's an indirect reference, but I'm sure you'll pick up on it."

This made me a little nervous. Rosh Hashanah is the Jewish New Year, a day on which to ponder one's mistakes of the previous year and consider resolutions for the next. I think one of the keys to my happiness is that I try to catch my mistakes and transgressions as quickly as possible after the fact and minimize the period of reflection. Was the rabbi going to bust me for something? Worse yet, was he going to do it in front of an entire congregation?

After a brief preamble about Jewish survival, the central theme of Rabbi Rubinstein's Rosh Hashanah message emerged: intermarriage. That is, marriage between those raised in the Jewish faith and those who are not. "I want to be clear about my position on this topic," he said. "There is no ambiguity. I urge Jews to marry Jews."

Uh-oh.

"The Jewish community seems to have a more certain future when Jews marry each other." He supported this by offering a few statistics, among which this stood out: "The chance of divorce terminating a marriage between a Jew and a non-Jew is twice as great as when two Jews marry."

I wouldn't characterize his tone as harsh or strident, just firm. But then he took a turn and began to speak about "matters of love" and the reality that given that "we want our children to grow up in multiracial, multiethnic, and multireligious environments," to then "tell our children that we don't want them to marry non-Jews" is a paradox. He went on to describe a hypothetical but incredibly familiar relationship between an interfaith couple, their attitudes and upbringing and the thinking behind their decisions about their religious convictions. He was remarkably perceptive and incredibly understanding. What I heard spoke directly to my experience and reinforced the positive feelings I have about the inclusive and empathetic quality of the Reform Jewish movement.

As he closed his remarks, Rabbi Rubinstein looked out at the congregation, paused briefly, and said, "Some of you are married to non-Jews . . . You are raising your children as Jews. Your spouse is standing beside you when your children are given their Hebrew names and when they become *bar/bat mitzvahs*. You've brought them to our family. You honor us and we reflect that honor back onto you. As I said at the beginning, I am passionately obsessed by Jewish survival. I believe that our future will be enhanced by bringing close our people's non-Jewish spouses and embracing those who choose to join us." His final stanza, I chose to take as the reference to me (and I'm sure many others in the sanctuary that day). "Let us be grateful to those who have chosen to be part of our destiny and our family. Let us throw open our doors to all who would choose to enter, and let us open our arms wide to embrace the non-Jews, those who are sitting among us today. They are precious and they are courageous and they are ours, and they are part of our future and our destiny. So let us all together, with them, be strong . . . with God's help. Amen."

Brothers and Sisters

I believe there is a higher power in this universe, and I know for a fact that it is not me. However, I still haven't found a religion or orthodoxy completely consistent with the way my heart and mind process this understanding. It's not that I am averse to accepted theologies. All of the folks I've talked about—Bishop Carlton Pearson, Russ and his wonderful family, Rabbi Rubinstein—rely on their faiths for strength, wisdom, and an ethical compass. Their beliefs are genuine and sincere, and I have tremendous respect for how their lives express those beliefs. My own experiences have instilled a belief that life is a gift. Recognizing that truth and being humbled by it makes me appreciate that I am a part of something great and timeless.

Parkinson's and alcohol took a sledgehammer to any illusions I may have had that I was in control. I came to accept that any disease or condition beyond my control is, in effect, a power greater than myself. To survive this destructive energy, I must look to an even higher power. For my purposes, I need neither define it nor have others define it for me, only accept its existence. It is evident in Tracy's love and inexhaustible friendship, the toothless gap in Esmé's smile, Aquinnah's grace, Schuyler's grit, Sam's intrepid curiosity. So much to savor, so much to be grateful for. And since I'm not sure of the address to which to send my gratitude, I put it out there in everything I do.

Chris Reeve wisely parsed the difference between optimism and hope. Unlike optimism, he said, "Hope is the product of knowledge and the projection of where the knowledge can take us." If optimism is a happy-go-lucky expectation that the odds are in my favor, that things are likely to break my way, and if hope is an informed optimism, facts converting desire into possibility, then faith is the third leg of the stool. Faith tells me that I'm not alone. And as my years with Parkinson's disease have taught me, if any of those legs is missing, I'm gonna fall on my ass. When going to sleep at night, I'm optimistic that I won't be awoken by a phone ringing with bad news. When the phone does ring, I hope it's a wrong number. When it's not and the caller has the worst news imaginable, it's time for faith to kick in. On November 5, 2007, the phone rang at 5:45 A.M. Tracy answered on the second ring and after a brief exchange, roused me with two simple words. "It's Steve."

At any decent hour of the day or night, one of my favorite people to hear from is my older brother. Steve is a great friend, a role model in the husband he is to his wife, the father he is to his children, the son he is to our mother, and the sibling he is to my sisters and me. He is also fiercely intelligent and flat-out funny—Bill Murray meets Steven Wright. He resides in a suburb of Vancouver, not far from the rest of my family (except for my sister, Kelli, a theater actress, who lives in Toronto), and I don't see him nearly enough. Tracy always chides me for my reluctance to spend more than a minute or two talking to anyone on the telephone. However, Steve is the exception. Swapping stories about our kids, telling jokes, and making plans for future reunions, we could sometimes shoot the shit for as long as an hour. But when the phone rings between midnight and 6:00 A.M., the last voice I want to hear on the other end of that line is Steve's. If something has gone horribly wrong on the West Coast and I need to be notified, it'll be big brother Steve who has to make the call.

I don't even like to see these words typed out on a page, but my first concern was for my mother. Mom is seventy-eight now, in robust health and typically sensational humor, and I'm fairly confident she'll outlast us all, but that's where your mind goes when the phone rings in the dark hours.

Eighteen years ago, my father died suddenly. Tracy and I and six-month-old Sam were living in California, and it was Steve, of course, who called to let us know that Dad had been rushed to the hospital and was not expected to make it. He was barely audible as he choked down sobs; it was a shitty job, but he was the only one who could have done it.

Almost eighteen years later in New York, with Tracy trailing behind me, I padded from our bedroom into the adjacent office to answer the phone. It was as though I knew I'd need to be standing for what I was about to hear.

"Mike?" asked the strained but familiar voice from thirty-two hundred miles away.

"What is it, Steve? What's happened? Is it Mom?"

"No," he said. "It's Karen."

Karen is the oldest of my three sisters. Eleven years older than I, she had already moved out of the house and started a family of her own when I was only eight. I saw plenty of her, her husband, Ed, and their two boys, Jamie and Richard, throughout my teenage years in BC. Obviously our contact diminished once I made my own move away to California at eighteen. Though our lives had changed dramatically, our connection remained strong. Karen, or K.C. as we call her (her middle name is Charlotte), had a rocky marriage, eventually divorcing her husband, who was later killed when struck by a car as he crossed a Vancouver street. Living in the States, I was raising a family of my own, and enjoying a lifestyle far removed from our shared childhood as military brats. What bonded us beyond the usual family ties was a shared tenacity, each of us having grown up with oversized personalities and undersized bodies. K.C. and I were the two shortest kids in our family—she was barely five feet. It was a physical imperative that we be always looking up, and this came to describe our attitudes toward life as well. Growing up (or not growing up) in a world of asses and elbows will make you either resilient or retiring, and Karen was no wallflower. Her temper was the stuff of legend. Whoever said "It's not the size of the dog in the fight but the size of the fight in the dog" must have met my little big sister. She'd rarely bite, but the only thing louder than her bark was her laugh.

My sister was tough as nails, taking on all comers, but her greatest battle was waged inside her own body. Karen was an epileptic. Seizures struck suddenly and dropped her where she stood, as often as two or three times a week. The problem progressed to the point where she could no longer drive and her whereabouts had to be accounted for at all times, lest dangerous surroundings or companions make a bad situation dire. When I was diagnosed with Parkinson's, our bond strengthened; we became the Bad-Brain Club. And even amid all the confusion of my early post-diagnosis days, our esprit de corps gave me a lot of comfort. Empathy is always better than sympathy, especially from family.

By 1993, epilepsy had begun to crush even Karen's spirits. The copious amounts of medication she had to take to suppress seizures deadened her to much of the joy in life. Though my Parkinson's demanded sacrifice and required that I take my own share of pharmaceuticals, her plight was growing desperate beyond anything I could relate to.

When she called one day to tell me she'd been accepted for

a somewhat unconventional and risky brain surgery to literally remove the part of her brain that was causing the seizures,
I was dubious. But any qualms I may have had were over-
whelmed by the unmistakable sense of hope she conveyed
that this procedure might be the answer to her prayers. My
youngest sister, Kelli, later recounted the conversation she'd
had when Karen told her the news of her plans.

"Are you sure you want to do this?" Kelli asked. "What if it
makes things worse?"

"It can't get any worse," K.C. replied.

"But still, isn't the devil you know better than the devil you
don't?"

Typical of Karen, her response was terse and matter of fact.
"You don't know my devil."

The surgery, it turned out, was a resounding success, and
during the next fifteen years, Karen, free from drugs and seizures, was back to her brash, funny, irrepressible self. I'm not
sure I would have had the guts to let doctors perform brain
surgery on me a few years later were it not for the intestinal
fortitude K.C. displayed in letting her own skull be cracked.
She got remarried to a slightly older (all right, he was almost
my mom's age) kilt-wearing Scotsman named Gordy, who
shared her quick laugh as well as a passion for golf. In addition
to the apartment they shared in the Vancouver suburbs, they
set up weekend housekeeping in a trailer park just across the
U.S. border, in the Washington state resort town of Birch Bay.
No one could have been more deserving of such happiness.

Just a few days prior to Steve's phone call, Karen had celebrated her fifty-seventh birthday. As with all my sisters, I had

a ritual of sending birthday flowers to Karen every October 27, and I always looked forward to the inevitable thank-you call that they inspired. Away for the weekend when the flowers arrived at her home, she didn't get back to me until the twenty-ninth. Our conversation was shorter than usual, but she thanked me profusely, and we shared a laugh or two. I distinctly remember saying I love you before I hung up. Less than a week later, I stood in the exact same place and talked with Steve on the exact same phone.

"They came home from Birch Bay," Steve was telling me. "Gordy said that Karen went out on the balcony to have a smoke, then came back in, passed by him on the way to the bathroom, and said she wasn't feeling well. A few seconds later, he heard a thump, went in to see what happened, and found Karen unconscious on the floor. Massive hemorrhaging in the brain. She hasn't woken up since."

I sank into the desk chair. "Where is she now?" I asked.

"She's in the hospital," Steve answered. "And, Mike, they don't think she's gonna wake up."

Much transpired in the twelve or so hours it took for me to book a flight and travel across North America to join my mother, siblings, Gordy, Richard, and Jamie at Karen's hospital bedside in Surrey, BC, none of it good. She was completely reliant on a respirator to keep her alive. Her brain, according to tests, was essentially dead; that is, she could survive, but only with a machine breathing for her and with no realistic chance that she could recover enough brain function to exist in anything more than a vegetative state.

I touched her hand and kissed her face, searching for some

small sign—an eye flutter, a shift in body weight, a finger twitch, anything. A look around at the faces of my family, though, told me that they had accepted what I was just beginning to grasp. K.C. was already gone. Nevertheless, we stood there for a few more hours until finally agreeing that we would all go home and get some rest. The doctors promised that they would perform another round of tests in the morning and confer with us at that time about the reality of Karen's situation.

My abrupt departure from New York and the uncertainty about what I was flying into had necessitated leaving Tracy and the kids behind. I missed Tracy terribly for the comfort and consolation she could have provided not only to me but also to the family she had become such an important part of. Sleep was not a possibility, so basically, I spent the night watching the clock, deciding that 5:00 A.M.—8:00 A.M. EST—would be a good time to call Tracy and fill her in on the sad details.

When we spoke, she asked if I'd like her to come out, and I found myself, for the first time, saying out loud what I knew in my heart to be true. "I think by the time you get here, she'll be gone. We're all meeting at the hospital to speak with the doctors. I'm pretty sure they're going to recommend that we let her go." What I could have said, but didn't, was that it might be best to wait until funeral plans were in place.

The outcome was certain, the doctor assured us, but the decision as to how to proceed was ours. We had collected in a small waiting room adjacent to the critical care unit, where Karen had spent the night. Families face moments like this, and I can't imagine how each of them arrives at the conclusion that is right for them and their loved ones. I can't even confidently recount how we arrived at ours. My brother, I know, rightly pointed out that Karen's life for the past fifteen years, post-surgery and post-seizures, had been such a reprieve for her that the prospect of the life that the doctors were describing would definitely not be what she'd choose for herself. It ultimately came down to a conversation between Gordy and my mom. It was brief and they both agreed. We would allow the hospital to turn off the respirator, and we'd spend the day saying our good-byes. A few minutes after the doctor accepted and affirmed our wishes, he returned, accompanied by a pleasant-looking woman in her mid- to late forties, who introduced herself as the hospital chaplain. She shook hands with each of us, sincerely offering her condolences. We hadn't requested clergy and were unsure of what to make of her presence. Mom, though, seemed comforted that God would be represented in this sad affair, even if by proxy. And so we invited the chaplain to remain with the family throughout whatever might unfold over the next few hours. I can't speak for anyone else, but I did feel a tinge of resentment, nothing like outrage, just the slightest feeling of being intruded upon. What do hospital chaplains do? Are they soul collectors? We had barely reconciled ourselves to the fact that we were losing someone we couldn't imagine being without, and she was there to what? Take the handoff for God? I wanted to hear what she had to say for herself.

I soon realized that my concerns were unfounded. She instinctively knew to go to my mom, and her affect was calming. Later, as we all gathered in Karen's private room, each of us somehow finding enough space around the bed to grip the rail in one hand and reach out with the other to touch K.C., the chaplain remained quiet. Hours passed, and the mood in the room did not grow more somber, as one might expect, but with every passing moment, each whispered good-bye, and each "We love you, K.C.," the vigil evolved into something intensely spiritual. We began to tell stories, share personal remembrances; there was laughter, even as we wiped tears with sleeves already soaked from previous buckets full. The hospital staff, which witnesses family tragedy on a daily basis, to my surprise, was not immune to the emotion and love being expressed by our family. The intervals between their visits shortened, and we knew that Karen's time with us was growing short.

She had barely spoken all afternoon, but now the chaplain stepped forward with a question. "Does Karen have a favorite song?"

Steve and I exchanged looks as a kind of alarm went off in my head. It occurred to me that she might suggest a hymn, and for some reason, I don't know why, this just seemed to me a little inappropriate.

"Something she loved as a teenager? Something she liked to sing?" the chaplain continued.

My sister Jackie, perhaps the most emotional of all of us throughout this ordeal, was the first to chime in, literally. In a soft, tremulous voice, she sang, *"Sweet little Sheila, you'll know her if you see her."*

Kelly joined in. *"Blue eyes and a ponytail."*

Tommy Roe, 1962. Karen loved that song. I'm sure none of

us even gave it much thought, but we all somehow knew the words. Even my brother and I could jump in on the chorus. *"We're so doggone happy, just bein' around together."*

Now everybody. *"Man that little girl is fine."*

We're crying, singing, and laughing. And K.C. is slipping away. And we're sad, but we know she's all right. We have faith.

· PART FOUR ·

Safe at Home

Cindy Gold

Lucky in Love

Just as people might assume that the period of eight years or so since I wrote the last book has been a period of diminishment, so might they assume that the same holds true for my married life, that as I have become enfeebled, my marriage has become encumbered. But, in fact, it has been a time of enlightenment that has led to tremendous enrichment.

Hey, that's not bad. I should have saved that for the card.

Today happens to be our twentieth wedding anniversary, and I've got a blank card that I have to fill with righteous sentiment sometime before dinner this evening—twenty years' worth of love, gratitude, affection, and respect in my own increasingly indecipherable cursive script. I promised myself I'd limit it to the two spaces within the card's fold.

Much of what has gone so right in the last twenty years has had to do with how what has gone wrong has been mitigated by our relationship, our partnership, our friendship, and in the broader sense, the possibility of a marriage done right. Sometimes people ask me the secret to a long and happy marriage, just as they ask me about the key to raising children. My flip answer in the kid department is "Love 'em, feed 'em, and keep 'em out of traffic." As for marriage, I often reply with equal brevity, "Keep the fights clean and the sex dirty." Of course, I don't really know the answer to either question, but what I have learned from my experiences in both areas is worth diving into more deeply. But first, let me take care of that card.

Love and Squalor

LOS ANGELES, CALIFORNIA · SEPTEMBER 11, 2001

The hotel phone woke me from a deep sleep. I wrestled the receiver from the cradle and saw that it was 6:00 A.M. I'd come to California to do a guest spot on the new Charlie Sheen version of *Spin City,* but I wasn't expected on set until 10:00 A.M. I mumbled something unintelligible.

"Turn on the television." It was Tracy.

"What? Yeah, sure, okay. What channel?"

"Doesn't matter, any channel."

Shit. That alone would have told me something was terribly wrong if I hadn't already intuited it from the early hour and the nervous quality of Tracy's voice. I hit the remote's on button, and as the television hummed to life, the tiny pixel at the center of the screen widened to reveal an image of the World Trade Center. A tremendous cloud of black smoke billowed from the tower on the right of the screen. The remote slipped from my hand. I rose from the bed, advancing trance-like toward the television until the clatter of the phone's base sliding off the nightstand, sweeping onto the floor my water glass, pill bottles, and *Spin City* script, reminded me that I still held the receiver.

"Am I seeing what I think I'm seeing?" I asked.

"There was an accident at the World Trade Center," Tracy said. "A plane hit one of the towers."

"I don't think this was an accident," I said. "They tried to blow it up in '93. What are they saying on TV?"

"I'm not sure," she said. "It just happened."

"Where are the kids?"

"Already at school."

Aquinnah and Schuyler were first graders at an Upper East Side school, relatively close to home and several miles north of Lower Manhattan, where events were unfolding. Sam, however, went to school downtown, not in the direct vicinity of the towers but certainly close enough to place him in the impact zone of a disaster of this magnitude.

"Wait a few minutes until we find out what's happening, but I think you should get ready to pull the kids out."

"All of them? The girls too?"

"I think so."

We were still on the phone when the second plane hit. The city where my children and my wife, eight months pregnant with our fourth child, were at this very minute was under attack. "Hang on a second," Tracy said. "That's the other line."

Before I could protest, she put me on hold. And after what seemed an interminable wait, though probably less than a minute, she was back. "You're not gonna believe who that was," she said. "It was Sy."

"Sy? The driver?" Sy worked for a New York–based livery company whose cars we sometimes used when an event or a situation called for a little more comfort and reliability than you could expect from a yellow cab. I liked Sy, a friendly, gravelly voiced older man, always with a story to tell. But for what I was about to hear from Tracy, he earned a spot in my heart forever.

"Sy has Sam," Tracy said. "He was in the neighborhood. And as soon as he heard about the second explosion, he went to school and picked him up. They're on their way home now. I'm gonna go get the girls. I'll call you back."

"Give Sy my number and have him call me," I said. Ten minutes later, on the TV in my Beverly Hills suite, I was witnessing a mass exodus, hundreds of thousands of people in cars and on foot, progressing northward along FDR Drive, some peeling off across each of the bridges on the East Side. What made the experience all the more frightening and surreal was that at that very moment my twelve-year-old son was speaking to me from the middle of the vast river of humanity as it carried him northward. He sounded frightened, but claimed he felt safe. However much reassurance his composure gave me, I knew I'd only feel better when they were all at home, or better yet, off the island of Manhattan altogether and up at our country place in Connecticut. Most desperately, of course, I wanted to be there with them—all of us together and safe.

I'm sure the emotional calculus proves true for a lot of people. With Tracy, my wife and mother of my children, I had developed a connection so profound that in an instant, I would put my own life at risk to protect hers. I would step in front of a train for her. With kids, a parent's train-defying protective instincts exist from day one. On September 11, 2001, while my family was in New York, I wasn't really in Los Angeles; if I was not with them, I was nowhere.

With each passing second, my resolve to get back to my family strengthened. But it quickly became obvious that there'd be no chance of catching a flight to New York, any alternative city on the Eastern Seaboard, or anywhere else in America, for that matter. The skies over the entire country had been shut down, closed for business.

In Los Angeles with me for the *Spin City* guest spot were Nelle Fortenberry, my producing partner, as well as Jackie Hamada, in just her first full week at work as my new personal assistant. Jackie's was a complicated job at the best of times, and these were quite suddenly the absolute worst of times. Nelle's husband, John, a television director, and their infant daughter, Tess, had also flown in earlier from New York.

I made several calls in between check-ins with Tracy and the kids, including a few back-and-forths with Jackie and a lengthy conversation with Nelle; though "conversation" might be a strong word. Each on his or her own end of the line, dumbstruck, we watched the news out of not just New York now, but also DC and Pennsylvania, occasionally interrupting the silence to offer interpretations of events. At that moment, millions around the country and across the world were doing the same thing: just trying to make some sense of it all.

"Have you heard from the production office?" she asked, in reference to the day's work schedule at *Spin City*.

"I don't know," I replied. "I've ordered a car."

For Nelle, this brought more confusion to what was already a very confusing morning. The studio provided me with transportation to and from work, so why would I need to arrange this? "A car and driver? To get to the studio?" she asked.

"I'm not going to the studio," I said. "I'm going to New York. It's Tuesday morning. If we only stop for gas, I can be there Thursday afternoon."

One of the things I love about Nelle is that she is so much more conscientious than I am. She was thinking about the production schedule. "So they're not doing the show this week?"

"I don't know. *I'm* not doing the show this week. *I'm* going home."

While slightly thrown, she understood my decision and said she'd call Gary Goldberg and let him know my plan. Jackie and I had initially discussed renting a car, though the two of us switching off at the wheel for forty-eight hours straight seemed a dubious proposition, and none of the car services we contacted was prepared to assign a vehicle and driver to make a three-thousand-mile trip into a war zone.

Gavin De Becker is a renowned personal security and threat assessment expert, as well as a personal friend. Years earlier, he had helped police and the DA track and prosecute a disturbed fan who had sent Tracy and me hundreds of death threats. Gavin's company also provided tabloid-thwarting security for our wedding and for other personal and public events over the years. I reached Gavin that morning, already hard at work, analyzing the situation in consultation with agencies to whom he had provided his expertise in the past. He was eager to assist me in any way possible. He agreed to provide an SUV, with two agents on driving detail.

We drove out of Los Angeles at approximately 3:30 P.M. The hotel's room service had prepared us some box lunches, and housekeeping provided pillows and blankets. I wouldn't be driving, but it was hard to imagine that I'd get much sleep.

Tracy decided that she would stay in our New York apartment. Friends in the neighborhood promised to be in close contact with her. I asked our friend Curtis Schenker, should the situation worsen, to relocate my family along with his own to our place in rural Connecticut. There was no guarantee, however, that they'd even be permitted to evacuate. Government concerns about follow-up attacks remained high, and traffic to and from Manhattan via the various bridges and tunnels had been severely restricted. We had been warned that we might arrive at the gates of the city only to be denied access, but as the saying goes, we would cross (or not cross) that bridge when we got to it. The important thing was getting to it.

Gavin's guys, Dennis and Steve, were all business, driving us through the Southwest, Texas, Oklahoma, up through Missouri, the Midwest, and into the Northeast. I agreed that tracing along the Rockies, while breathtakingly scenic, would add extra miles and eat up the clock. Once we were out of Los Angeles, cell phone reception was spotty. Whenever I could find and maintain a signal, I'd call Tracy, the same way a marathon runner continually checks his pulse. From region to region, we were able to find NPR on the radio with only an occasional adjustment of the dial. The mood in the car was somber. We made a few stops for gas and food, including, at one point, a plate of spaghetti at a Texas Panhandle Olive Garden. This was my fourth time crossing the country by car; just four years earlier I had made the trip with Sam. But whereas Sam and I had sought out diversity in the American experience, this time around I felt comforted by the sameness, the carbon copy quality of the culture. I knew that I was tasting the spaghetti at every Olive Garden in the country. The patrons at the restaurant were as focused on the events of New York and Washington as I imagine the people in New Jersey were. Stopping to use the restroom at a state-run tourist information kiosk in Oklahoma, we saw a makeshift sign that pronounced, "All government agencies closed until further notice due to terrorist threat." I doubt Al Qaeda had that two-seat outhouse and map stand in their crosshairs, but I saw it as a gesture of solidarity rather than a response to an immediate threat. Passing through Oklahoma City reminded me of the homegrown terror just six years earlier when the Federal Building was destroyed, killing nearly two hundred people. I remembered an image of a fireman carrying a wounded baby and thinking that it couldn't get much worse than that. I realized now that when it gets bad, it's just bad. There are no degrees. Early in the morning on September 13 we rolled through St. Louis. I couldn't decide whether the iconic Gateway Arch seemed vulnerable or defiant—both, I guess. That dichotomy summed up the mood of this country that I was slipping through like a ghost.

By late afternoon, we were in Somerset County, Pennsylvania, very close to the tract of rural farmland where, just two days before, a group of passengers on a plane bound from Newark to San Francisco forced a crash into Pennsylvania soil rather than be diverted to the White House. I called Tracy to let her know how far we'd come and how soon I would be home. She had a request: could I pick up a loaf of bread?

By dusk, we were in New Jersey. Across the Hudson River, Manhattan, shrouded in smoke, dust, and ash, was barely visible. The absence of the towers was the most prominent feature on the landscape. The sky gave me the impression of a fresh bruise. Staring at it was painful, though I couldn't stop.

Dennis and Steve, unfamiliar with traffic patterns in, out of, and around Manhattan, overshot the turnpike exit. We doubled back to the George Washington Bridge, the only viable route into the city from the west. One last stop for gas, and per Tracy's request, I bought a loaf of bread. We joined a long queue of cars and trucks being combed over by security personnel, both police and military. Forty-eight hours and change had passed since we'd left Los Angeles, and having arrived, I felt gut-struck by what I had come back to find. To paraphrase the song, I really felt as though I was coming home to a place I'd never been before.

My only concrete wish upon being reunited with my family was to hold all three of the kids as long as they could stand it, and by holding Tracy, embrace our fourth child, due in less than two months. I refloated my plan to move us all out of the city, at least on a temporary basis. New York, or so the radio had been reporting, expected more attacks; government services were limited, and as I gathered from Tracy's bread request, merchants were dealing with interrupted supply lines.

Having had their sense of security bolstered by my return, the kids didn't want to go to Connecticut; they didn't want to go anywhere. What they wanted was to get back to school and be with their friends. I expected that Tracy, in the late stages of her pregnancy, would feel differently and want to escape from

New York. But she too felt that it was best for both our family and our city that we stay put.

Two days in the car with no access to television had exposed me to few of the unforgettable images replayed over the last two days. Indelibly imprinted on my mind, of course, were images of the initial cataclysm: buildings folding in on themselves, terrified people fleeing through skyscraper canyons, pursued by roiling clouds of death. But now I was getting a chance to witness firsthand the courage, bravery, self-sacrifice, and enveloping sense of community present from the moment the first plane hit. I began to understand why so many stayed. Many were fearful, but so too were they hopeful. The effects reverberated nationwide, but while New York had been laid low by the most despicable acts, by the most awful suffering human beings could inflict upon other human beings, it had also been buoyed by its greater virtues. Hope, in this case, truly was optimism informed by the knowledge that more people were inclined to do good than to do evil.

MOUNT SINAI HOSPITAL, NEW YORK CITY
NOVEMBER 3, 2001

Less than two months later, Tracy delivered to us a fourth child, a third daughter. We named her Esmé after the title character in J. D. Salinger's "For Esmé—with Love and Squalor." "Love and squalor" seemed an apt description for what we'd experienced in the preceding weeks. On November 4, 2001, just a few hours before we brought Esmé to our home, I stood by the window in Tracy's hospital room and looked out upon an incredible scene unfolding below on Fifth Avenue. The New York City Marathon, an event threatened with cancellation, was proceeding in high style. This was an altogether different kind of explosion: an explosion of color, energy, and endurance, a true celebration of human spirit. Esmé's first look at her city and at her world was, for her, more love than squalor.

Why I'm Still with Tracy and Shaky When I'm Not

COLUMBIA UNIVERSITY, NEW YORK
SEPTEMBER II, 2008

Seven years later, in commemoration of the events of September 11, 2001, presidential candidates Barack Obama and John McCain came to Columbia University in New York to speak separately—though from the same stage and on the same night—on the topic of public service. Columbia's campus is just across Central Park and a dozen or so blocks north of our home, so we decided to watch the proceedings in person rather than on television. Leonardo DiCaprio and Tobey Maguire occupied the seats directly in front of us. A few seats down, Jon Bon Jovi anchored the row, and immediately to my left sat R & B superstar Usher Raymond.

Minutes into the program, though, I wished we had stuck with the TV option. My regret had nothing to do with what I was hearing from the introductory speakers. My mind was fully engaged; the problem was with my brain. With relatively little warning, I began to shake dramatically, bouncing on my seat and alternating between folding my flailing arms in front of me and pinning my hands to my seat with my butt. The ominous development, however, was the way my legs were freaking out. Extending them straight out in front of me, I pressed them together, as if to fuse them into one more manageable limb rather than two independently rebellious ones. This put me in real danger of kicking Spider-Man in the ass, but when I flattened them against the floor, this set them off, tapping and skidding from side to side, which risked Usher mistaking my little dance as a Senator Larry Craig "wide-stance" flirtation. If I had a moment to escape, it vanished when John McCain took the stage.

"I knew it was as bad as it gets," Tracy told me later, "and you really needed to walk it off, just be alone until your pills kicked in. But I worried that you'd be forced to bolt out of your chair while McCain was speaking and the Secret Service would tackle you to the ground."

When Judy Woodruff, one of the evening's moderators, along with Time magazine managing editor Richard Stengel, threw to commercial at the end of McCain's first segment, Tracy saw this as the break I needed. For reasons that are difficult to explain after the moment, I voiced reluctance when she offered to walk me out of the auditorium. While movement is initially difficult, committing to a simple action is even more difficult, and having Tracy usher me past Usher might be even more embarrassing than my wide-stance Larry Craig footsie—I could easily end up in the guy's lap.

Despite my wife's best efforts to get me up and out, I hemmed and hawed, wavered and quavered through the bulk of the break and tried to convince her that the pills were beginning to work their magic and that relief was imminent. But when the stage lights came up again, as if on cue, the tremors worsened, and I steeled myself for *another round. Isometrically transferring energy from one part of my body to another is intense labor, like putting out a house fire with teaspoons of water, and I dripped sweat. Seeing the rivulets trickle from hairline to jawline, Tracy reached over to remove my suit jacket, but after easing it over my shoulders, she hesitated and slid it back on. My powder blue dress shirt was stained indigo with perspiration. At the next brief intermission, after what seemed like an eternity, I allowed her to lead me out.*

In less than a minute, I was in the quiet corner of an anteroom, guzzling a cold bottle of water. I had urged Tracy to go back to her seat; she promised to come back and check on me at the intermission before Obama took the stage. I spent the next ten minutes mulling over how lucky I am.

Except for the fact that at some point we were both in the same room as the next President of the United States, that evening wasn't really so unusual. Parkinson's is always putting me in a box, and Tracy has become an expert at folding back the flaps, tipping it over, and easing me out. This doesn't escape notice and has quite rightly earned her a great deal of respect as well as the empathy of others who have found themselves in caretaker roles. Understandably, people project their situation onto hers. And while she's always gracious and feels a great deal of compassion for those who struggle, it is not a role that she is particularly comfortable in. She just doesn't see it that way. Not that being married to me is a piece of cake—it does require coping skills—but she would quickly tell you, probably with a laugh, that the greatest challenge she faces is not having a Parkinson's patient for a husband, it's having *me* for a husband. And by the way, I am a Parkinson's patient.

Sam always struggled with basic arithmetic, but as his education progressed, he inexplicably proved to be excellent at math—sounds like a contradiction, but it's not. While the basic stuff—quick addition, multiplication tables, long division— seemed to baffle him, when he had more complex processes to master—algebra, trig, calculus—he thrived. I think Tracy and I feel the same way about marriage. The more complicated it gets, the more it seems to bring out the best in us.

Confronted with a complication as seemingly dire as my PD diagnosis, so early on in our marriage, could have left us undone. I, for one, was not a willing supplicant to reality. I was a big believer in my own press: a happy-go-lucky lottery winner who'd had it all—a great career, a beautiful wife, a healthy son. I was struggling, though, with figuring out how to keep it all going. I was working more than I needed to, worrying more than I liked to admit, and drinking more than anyone should. I was, to put it mildly, not well positioned to deal with what was coming.

Over the course of her own life, Tracy had developed a number of character traits that, while helpful in the past, would be no use to her now and, at worst, counterproductive. She is a firm believer that careful research and meticulous planning can help avert any disaster. When I learned shortly after meeting her that she was a bit of a hypochondriac, I thought it was cute, but I couldn't relate—getting seriously sick was something that happened to other people. The change that Parkinson's itself has forced upon me and, by extension, Tracy and the family, pales in comparison to the changes we have brought upon ourselves. We give more to each other than Parkinson's could ever take away.

For Tracy and me, it would be hard to separate our personal growth from the growth of our family. After my PD diagnosis, some people actually expressed shock and concern when we told them of our plans to have more kids. "Is that fair?" they asked. "Fair to the kid? Fair to you? What about the future?" I know what kind of bleak fate they'd envisioned for me, but I'm happy to say, it hasn't materialized.

So after Sam came the twins, Schuyler and Aquinnah, and six years later, Esmé.

The Family Plan

There's a truism about parenting that goes like this: When your first baby is sucking on a pacifier and spits it out onto the floor, you pick that pacifier up, and before returning it to your child's mouth, you immerse it in boiling water to make sure you've destroyed any traces of bacteria. With your second child, you realize a quick pass under a stream of warm tap water will do the trick. With your third child, you pick the pacifier up off the floor, lick it yourself, and pop it back in the kid's mouth. With the fourth, you let the dog lick it.

To those curious as to why Tracy and I, parents with three children, would have another child in our forties, we offer these reasons:

"The house wasn't quite noisy enough yet."

"Our kitchen table seats six."

"We just had this feeling that someone was still missing."

In simple terms, I guess you could say that we, as a family, weren't "there" yet. Another way of looking at it is that, personally, I was more "there" at the time of Esmé's birth than at the time of any of the previous three. *Back to the Future Part II* and *Part III*, *The Hard Way*, *Doc Hollywood*, *For Love or Money*, *Life with Mikey*, and *Greedy*—I made seven films before Sam turned five. And in the first four years of the twins' lives, I was starring in and producing a weekly television series. I was ten years out from my Parkinson's diagnosis and into my first year of retirement from *Spin City* when Esmé was born. I would be there to hear her first words, to see her first steps; I would come to see the richness and depth of her character.

If Esmé would have shared the pacifier with our dog, Daisy, you could say that Sam, born less than a year after Tracy and I were married, spent a lot of time waiting for the proverbial water to boil. As first-time parents, Tracy and I fell into a pattern, going completely overboard on what, in retrospect, were the most basic elements of the process. We attended countless Lamaze and early parenting classes (diapering rubber dolls, etc.). We'd react to every cry and whimper like it was an air raid siren, unconvinced for some reason that a regular pattern of breathing could be maintained by this spectacularly healthy baby. Rarely away from us, Sam came on vacations and to business meetings and restaurants. If either of us was working, on-set accommodations were arranged. Crib-side vigils were a nightly ritual, ostensibly in case he cried for a bottle, or produced more frightening noises calling for a diaper change. Really, it was just to make sure he was still alive, a continuing miracle.

"Miracle" isn't too strong a word for a young father to use. My feeling was (and I know others harbor this same delusion) that this baby, *our* baby, had special significance. Just as every bride on her wedding day is Grace Kelly before she realizes that maybe she didn't marry a prince, and she's living in Bayonne, New Jersey, not Monaco; so do all first-time parents think they've delivered the Christ Child. The sooner they realize their error, the better for Junior. Scores of books and cable television shows feed this parental narcissism. Of course, there's no single correct way to care for a baby or raise a child. Even the most well-meaning, by-the-book mom or dad can, at some point in the day, commit a colossal screwup.

When Sam was born, I traded in my Ferrari, a twelve-cylinder, two-seat, screaming, black death machine, for an ultrasafe, top-end, family-style SUV. We consulted *Consumer Reports* magazine to find the baby seat with the highest test rating and dutifully installed it. One day after a playdate (well, I guess Sam was only five months old, so how much of a date could it have been?), I was driving my young family home along Mulholland Drive, negotiating the treacherous curves with extreme caution. Sam was quietly cooing in the back, and Tracy and I were engrossed in our conversation, probably all about Sam's obvious brilliance relative to his clearly non–Christ Child playmate. We pulled into our driveway, turned to the backseat, and Sam was gone. We panicked. Both of us scrambled past each other to be first to find him. And there was Sam, still cooing happily, upside down in the footwell behind the passenger seat. He was still securely strapped into his expensive car seat, only it had never been securely fastened to the expensive car. It's almost funny now—well, not quite—but at the time, we were horrified.

We pored over Sam for any sign of injury and wondered, quite seriously, if there might be any long-term psychological damage, any psychic trauma to go along with the physical. We may have argued for days about whose fault it was; whether I, being the driver, had the ultimate responsibility to make sure my passengers were secure, or if precisely because I was driving, that was something Tracy could easily have taken care of herself. We asked our friends, other young parents, if they'd had any similar experiences and fell flush with guilty embarrassment when they answered, "Well, no," and rather insincerely added, "But you shouldn't worry about it." Suffice it to say that it never happened again. From that day on, the key never turned in the ignition until we knew the seat was strapped in.

Of course, were the same thing to happen now with Esmé, we'd check to make sure that she was okay and, seeing that she was, share a collective "Well, that happened," and go straight to the part about making sure it never happened again.

As a frequent guest on both of David Letterman's shows, I found that I could always get a few cheap laughs out of Dave by telling stories about my kids and my various adventures in parenting. This was especially true during the show's first incarnation on NBC, when Sam was in the infant and toddler stages. Parenthood flummoxed Dave. It seemed to him an occupation fraught with more risk than reward.

"Sure," he would say, "little kids are cute and everything, but I just don't get what you do with them."

I sensed that what Dave was getting at was a bachelor's aversion to the endless responsibilities of raising a child, and I decided to feed his anxiety by playing into it. "Well, Dave," I responded, "hanging out with Sam or any two-year-old is basically one big suicide watch. Their mission is to find one new way after another of offing themselves—piss in an electric socket, lick a pit bull's nose, chase an ice cream truck into traffic—and your job as a parent is to step in before it happens."

Overprotectiveness can be a hard concept for a young parent of an only child to grasp. In addition to the constant vigilance, or "suicide watch" as I described it to Dave, Tracy and I had our home baby-proofed. Beyond just putting sharp objects, medicines, household poisons, and other hazards safely out of reach, we had every coffee table corner padded, every wall socket plugged, and every open door and stairway barricaded with a folding gate. I don't remember this degree of accident prevention when I was a kid. Who could afford it? I do recall one method of keeping children out of harm's way employed by a few mothers on the army bases where I grew up. They would place their toddler in a safety harness tethered to a clothesline in the backyard.

As I see it, Mom's more free-range approach to child safety was neither careless nor negligent as much as Darwinian. She took her chances, or our chances, and even she'd have to admit that the results were mixed. I stumbled, tumbled, slammed, and slid my way into more dangerous predicaments by the time I was six than I think Sam has in his entire life. An apartment complex we once lived in had a concrete retaining wall around the parking lot. The shortcut I used to take from my friend's apartment to ours involved zipping around a corner of that wall at high speeds. My mother could have been right there every time I barreled by, warning me to keep my head up, but eventually, I still would have run into the corner of that wall with enough force to fracture my skull and split my head open for fourteen stitches. In the absence of mothers, concrete walls are persuasive teachers. I was the fourth of five kids. Both of my parents worked, Dad often away on some military posting, so I was on my own a lot. If the freedom I enjoyed came at the price of chipped teeth, some stitches, and the occasional concussion, it was worth it.

If all the risks are removed from a child's environment, the child will be doomed to a life of playing it safe. Ironically, it was when the twins arrived, and Sam's world became more crowded, that he suddenly had more room to move. If Tracy had been pregnant with only one child, perhaps we could have remained as watchful over both children.

It's not likely that Sam would have taken up surfing, skiing, and scuba diving, or have made the decision to attend college in California, the width of a continent away from the comforts of home, had we continued to guard his every step.

Over the past nineteen years, I have come to understand that no parent can get his or her arms around all of the could've, would've, should'ves, mights, maybes, and what-ifs. Each new moment gives you a sufficient load to carry, and I've learned, especially as my arms have grown shakier, that there are times when the wisest thing to do is to let go.

Letting go doesn't just mean eschewing the unpleasant stuff, it also means knowing when something is not yours to hold. Aquinnah, my oldest daughter (by ten minutes), is a classically trained ballerina. Fourteen years old, she's been at it since preschool. Aquinnah is willowy—not just visually, but also in the muscular flexibility that allows her to bend but never break. Tracy had a background in ballet too, but she would be the first to admit that Aquinnah's passion and progress is beyond what she ever aspired to. She's introducing us to experiences we'd never have if we called all the shots.

Middle of the row, orchestra section of the New York State Theater in Lincoln Center, I sit next to Tracy. Esmé, rapt, shares both our laps as we approach the moment in *The Nutcracker* when the impossibly gigantic woman parts the pleats of her hoop skirt, releasing a dozen or so tiny dancers, who emerge and flit across the stage. My focus is on the third from the left—little, ethereal, ecstatically happy. I'm more at home at the ball game than the ballet, but I'm feeling completely at home right now; not my home—Aquinnah's.

Schuyler danced for a few years too. She was accepted into the same prestigious school of ballet along with her sister, and has appeared onstage in a few professional productions herself. Two years ago, she came to us and said she'd really like to try something else, sports maybe. For twins, the life of each is inextricably connected to the other's. Gaining footholds outside of the security and mysterious enigma of being one-half instead of one's own are daunting steps. Schuyler's feet just feel better in soccer boots than toe shoes; cartwheeling the length of a gym mat excites her more than scissor-leaping the width of a stage. I let go of any last remaining delusion that nothing major could transpire in this kid's heart, between her ears, or in her soul without my having put it there, when I saw her run the 100m.

From my seat in the near-empty bleachers of Icahn Stadium, I follow the little blond-and-blue dot that is Schuyler in her track uniform as she bounces in and around the infield and then back and forth across the track between heats. She congratulates one of her teammates, though knowing Sky, she really pays little or no attention to who wins or loses. Several New York City independent schools are represented, and the competition appears formidable. Schuyler leaves a gaggle of her friends mid-giggle and proceeds to the far end of the track, where runners are lining up for the 100m, Schuyler's event. Because of her small stature, I lose her intermittently behind the taller, more mature-looking girls in the first few races, but when I do get a glimpse of her, she seems happy, smiling as usual, and completely unaware and unconcerned that she is about to compete. I walk half the length of the bleachers to the midway point between the start and finish lines. Does she know how to do this? Standing still at the line while the competitors on either side of her shake out their long limbs to loosen and warm them up, Sky looks like a lamb before the slaughter. The only thing holding me back from shouting out advice is that I have little or no practical advice to offer, knowing only slightly more about racing than I know about dancing—in other words, not much. The starter raises the gun. Sky looks down, then up, and that half second is transforming. Her cherubic face looks lean and stoic; her eyes narrow to gun slits. *Jesus,* I think as the pistol cracks, *she's going to win this.* And she does. It isn't even close.

Esmé, as she is our fourth child, was never an only child like Sam, or connected physiologically and psychologically to a sibling in the way that the twins were and are.

This scene, or a version of it, has played out countless times in our household over the last few years: I'm sitting at the kitchen banquette in our New York City apartment, reading the paper, having a bite to eat, or helping one of the older kids with homework, and Esmé passes through. She moves with a sense of purpose. She offers no greeting, but I manage to sputter out a quick "Hey, Ez," and her hand, the last part of her to exit through the door on the other side of the room, gives me a friendly, if dismissive, wave. A few minutes later she comes back in through that same door, only now she is carrying a stuffed animal, a roll of duct tape, and an egg carton. I know she's going to come through again. When she does, she is wearing a raincoat, flip-flops, and a pair of cheap Disney elasticized fairy wings. She seems to be reading instructions out of a book. The next time through, I don't even look up. I just ask her a one-word question: "Cockamamie?"

"Yep," she answers, with just a quick glance in my direction. "It's a cock-a-mamie—a good one."

"Cockamamie," as in "cockamamie scheme," is an expression Tracy first applied a few years ago to any and all of the various eccentrically imaginative plans hatched by Esmé, in part to entertain others, but mostly to amuse herself. It might be an elaborate show she's staged in her cramped bedroom, employing the talents of her hundreds of stuffed animals or any live warm body who happens to be nearby at the moment of inspiration. It could be a song that she's written or a dance that she's choreographed, a book that she's illustrated or a teetering tower of a sculpture that she's assembled in the bathtub.

Esmé's creativity is definitely nature over nurture. She's an old soul; I often describe her as someone who's "been here before." Lazy New Age thinking perhaps, but she did seem to have arrived with a built-in familiarity to handle the basics and beyond. She is curious, inventive, creative, and fall-down funny—she is who I always wanted to be when I grew up. The trick she's mastered, or maybe it's more of a facility than a trick, is moving effortlessly between the boundless world of her imagination and the everyday world the rest of us occupy. She's not an escapist; she just holds two passports and travels often. I always warn babysitters, teachers, visiting relatives, or anyone else looking to occupy Esmé with one activity or another, "If you come upon her lying flat on her back on the sofa, on a rug, or in a tree branch, her eyes staring into space while her right hand teases the hair behind her ear into a ringlet, she's not doing *nothing*. She's *busy*. Let it go."

· · ·

I hate to say it, but I know parents who regard their children as instruments to be played. It's all a matter of what strings to pull and how finely they're tuned. I see them, to extend the metaphor, more as jukeboxes. Put in your two bits, maybe give them a bit of a nudge to get them going, but nine times out of ten, if you're lucky, they're going to play their own tune. That has consistently been the thrill for Tracy and me. To discover what they've discovered, to hear them recount their joys and successes, to let them have full ownership of all they've accomplished, and credit themselves for what they've learned, is the best and easiest part of parenting for me.

It's much harder, however, to let them own their failures and disappointments. The truth is, of course, that you have no choice. To some extent, the load can be shared, but it can never entirely be taken away.

This experience will be familiar to any parent, and Tracy and I have been through it with our four kids at least a dozen times: crouching in a bathroom at three o'clock in the morning, holding a damp cloth to the forehead of a young child who, having no idea what just hit him or her, retches from a kneeling position into the toilet bowl, simultaneously shivering and sweating. The drama will probably be reprised three or four times over the course of the night. No one will get any sleep. The sheets are off the bed in a sticky rumpled pile by the washing machine because the first time it happened you were too groggy to realize why the kid was waking you so urgently. Between purges, you pop in a thermometer to see if the fever has broken. The younger the age, the more you ache for the child. All the while, you supply a running commentary: "I know, baby. It's all right. Almost done. This is the last time. It'll be okay."

But this isn't what you want to say. What you really want is to rock your head back and shout, "For Christ's sake, please, give it to me. Let me take it." But you don't do that, because you can't do that. It doesn't work that way. And I'm just talking everyday garden-variety sickness here. We all know that there are parents who wish that this were all they had to watch their children endure. Their ordeals are unthinkable. Those of us who are blessed to have children who remain whole, healthy, and happy can at least appreciate these late nights in the bathroom as relatively gentle reminders that you can't take away your child's pain. You can only be present, be aware, be responsive, be compassionate, and love that child with everything you have.

Of course, my forty-seven years, my childhood, the ups and downs of my career, my experience with and ultimate surrender to alcohol, my diagnosis and subsequent life with Parkinson's disease, as well as everything before, after, and in between, have taught me something about resiliency. No matter how well intentioned, if I somehow convinced my children that I could remove their problems and relieve their pain, spare them the ups and downs of life, I'd be doing them a huge disservice.

SEPTEMBER 2008

My dad's formal education extended into the ninth grade, although he'd quickly remind you that he graduated magna cum laude from the School of Hard Knocks. Myself, I made it to the eleventh grade, and in fact, in the spring of what would have been my senior year, while my erstwhile classmates were taking finals, I was being chauffeured by my father in his old Dodge down to Los Angeles to find an agent.

It's not that pursuit of knowledge wasn't always encouraged in my family; it's just that we didn't assume that a structure would automatically be in place to support that process. Tracy comes from a highly educated family. Among her immediate family are past and present teachers, professors, accomplished writers, and successful entrepreneurs. In fact, the only one who didn't attend college was Tracy. She was accepted into the university of her choice, but postponed her attendance while she tried acting school and attempted to get her career off the ground. As her acting career took off, her plans for college faded.

For various reasons, however, I always assumed that Sam would attend college; certainly the independent schooling he'd received throughout his life was designed to prepare each student for that eventuality. I predict that if you compared the percentage of college-bound to non-college-bound students at Sam's high school and mine, the percentages would be inverse of one another. Well, that's not completely true; I believe 100 percent of the graduates from Sam's school are attending college, whereas only a handful of my peers went off to higher education, with the exception of the occasional trade school.

Last fall, my son, Sam, left for California to attend Stanford University. Because he's my firstborn and my only son, Sam has been subject to more projection and idealization than any of my other children. The temptation is always there to view his journey through the lens of my own experience. I've become especially aware of this because, as the son of a well-known father, Sam has the added burden of other people's projections, aside from my own.

The expectation that Sam has always had to deal with, I suppose, is that because I'm a well-known actor, he would choose the same career. Aside from raising his hand to be the magician's assistant at his sixth birthday party, Sam has never expressed an interest in showbiz. If there is such a thing as a typical "celebrity" kid, Sam does not fit the mold. Over the last ten years or so, especially, we have lived our lives away from the spotlight, but if he were inclined to bask in any spillover glow, he's had plenty of opportunity; it's just not his style.

Sam went off to college not to be a theater major, but rather to pursue his interests in math and science. I'm sure that his own vision of how his college career will unfold is still inchoate. He has talked about going into medical research, with a particular focus on cellular biology. When I tell this to people, I often get the same reaction. I can see them putting the story together in their own minds before they look to me for confirmation.

"Medical research, you mean, like Parkinson's research?" they ask.

I see where they want me to go. It is a romantic notion, far more compelling than another father-son acting duo. I wait to answer, let them think about it for a minute to the point where I can almost see the tears welling in the corners of their eyes.

"Hey, I'd be happy if he cured baldness."

I haven't pushed Sam here. I let him go.

Are We There Yet?

CANADIAN FORCES BASE CHILLIWACK,
BRITISH COLUMBIA · 1968

In 1968, my army sergeant father received notice that he was being transferred from his present posting at the Chilliwack base in British Columbia to the NORAD NATO military installation in North Bay, Ontario. For my mom and dad and the eldest three of my four siblings, this wasn't good news. To my dad, the notice seemed to come from out of the blue. It seemed punitive and, at best, capricious on the part of the army brass. Being a twenty-year veteran, he resented being forced to relocate his family two thousand miles across the country, after having moved them around so many times already—three times since I was born and many more before that. For my older brother and sisters, well settled into high school, it meant severing friendships and interrupting their academic lives. My baby sister, Kelli, just a bit older than I was back in '64 when my family made our last big move from Edmonton, Alberta, across the Rockies to BC, was oblivious to the upheaval. To me, it was all a big adventure—my first Great Road Trip.

Whatever the whys and wherefores of our family's eastward migration, it's how we did it that still seems to me a miracle on the order of "the fishes and the loaves." We did have a big-ass automobile—a royal blue 1967 Pontiac Laurentian, four doors, with bench seats in front and back and a rented U-Haul carryall box strapped to the roof. The trunk was so filled past capacity, Dad had to secure the lid with rope to keep it from flapping open and spilling the flotsam and jet-sam of our lives all over the Trans-Canada Highway. Inside the car, my father drove; my mom rode shotgun; and three-year-old Kelli occupied the space between them. In the back were my sister Karen (eighteen), my brother, Steve (fifteen), my sister Jackie (twelve), and me, scrapping over every square inch of vinyl.

Cars of that vintage did come equipped with seat belts, but they were of the lap-belt variety and were rarely used; I know we didn't bother with them. Wait, that's not strictly true. Somewhere in the vicinity of Moose Jaw, Saskatchewan, after a pitched battle over a torn Jughead comic book, I swung the metal business end of one into Jackie's head with sufficient velocity to open a gash just behind her ear. Such a ruckus, having escalated to actual bloodshed, had Mom reaching over the backseat in a vain effort to separate us. My dad, en-sconced behind the wheel in his short-sleeved checked pen-guin shirt, his tattooed arm crooked out the open driver's side window so that he collected a vicious sunburn on only the tip of his elbow, would bark out something scary, and under the circumstances, preposterous, like "Don't make me come back there!" If it had been a pleasure trip and not one inspired by professional necessity, he might have said, "I'll turn this goddamn car around right now!" But that was equally impossible, much to his chagrin.

With gas prices well below the fifty-cent-per-gallon mark and our accommodations provided by the oversized army-issued canvas tent carried in the roof-mounted U-Haul box and hastily pitched at campgrounds in towns like Peapod or

Flin Flon, expenses were minimal. I'm fairly sure, however, that they exceeded whatever exiguous travel allowance the army had provided. Each morning the tent came down before the sun came up, and we'd be off. There were at least a couple of reasons for this, one being that, like most cars at that time, ours lacked air-conditioning, and we wanted to get as many miles in as we could before the Pontiac became a rolling soup pot of sweat, stink, and surliness brought to a boil in the afternoon heat. Another had more to do with pleasure than practicality. By hitting the road early, we'd arrive in the next town and set up the tent with enough daylight to explore the local environs—a beach, a playground, or if we were lucky, some tacky roadside attraction like a reptile petting zoo/gas station or a petrified forest. Canada's proximity to the North Pole means that even the earliest days of summer can last until well into the evening, with dusty blue skies as late as 10:30 P.M. Maybe this is why my childhood seems to have lasted so long, while that of my own children seems so fleeting.

Dad had certain rules of the road that we as passengers (or human cargo, as I'm sure he preferred to think about us at times) were conditioned to abide by. My mom, the navigator, was expected to be aware of the route for any particular day, be familiar with that section of the correct map, and when called upon, relay the info to Dad clearly and succinctly. At no time was anyone to suggest that a fellow motorist, café waitress, or gas station attendant should be consulted for advice. Dad's nightmare was that he'd ask some local at a fork in the road if it made a difference which way we went to get to Winnipeg, for example, and would be told smugly, "Not to me, it doesn't." Mom wasn't allowed to tell Dad if he was clear to make a left onto a busy street, but if he pulled out too soon or too late, narrowly averting collision, she was to blame. It made for tense travel.

As for us kids, we didn't even think about participating in any way with Dad's driving, wisely remaining silent for long stretches of time. Speaking of stretching—"getting out to stretch" was reserved for lunch breaks or bathroom stops. As to the former, the Canadian roadscape in 1968 featured the occasional McDonald's, Dairy Queen, or Kentucky Fried Chicken, but roadside eateries were mostly geographically specific—in other words, local joints. There was nowhere near the proliferation of plastic road signs announcing the ubiquity of franchise food chains, a phenomenon we would not see until our return trip three years later. If we did pass a Burger King or a Dairy Queen, that's exactly what we would do—pass. The budget didn't allow for much beyond the foil-wrapped cold cuts on white bread and Tupperwared coleslaw that Mom had thrown together in camp that morning and tucked into our Coleman cooler.

More than a stop for fast food, my deepest desire was for Dad to pull into somewhere, anywhere, with a bathroom—any stanky, fly-ridden, heavily attended but lightly attended-to truck stop shithouse would do. Just to be allowed to stand in the breakdown lane of the Trans-Canada Highway, bare-assed to the passing parade, while I released the dam and soaked an Alberta scrub pine, would have been far better than a Big Mac.

I never understood my father's dogged aversion to the bathroom stop. In part, I guess, it had something to do with his belief that the world's worst calamities could befall you only if you were foolish enough to exit the freeway. The specter of getting lost on the byways and back roads of rural Canada was reason enough to suffer the searing pain to the kidneys and bladder that came with denying the compulsion to pee. Fierce backseat negotiations were enjoined in an effort by one or two of us to rally a declaration of solidarity to implore my father to pull off the highway. My dad's answer was that we should synchronize our urges. He never had to stop, which is amazing considering the amount of coffee he'd consume in a day. Wriggling, squirming, and crossing our legs, we'd try to distract ourselves by perusing a ratty *Mad* magazine for the thousandth time or by playing another round of punch buggy, which involved pounding your fist into the shoulder of the person next to you at the sight of a Volkswagen, so common that each of us bore purple bruises. Luckily my mother needed frequent pit-stops. We'd always push the coffee on her in the morning, as she was not as immune to its diuretic properties as my father.

The surest way to aggravate Dad to the point of apoplexy was to utter the words "Are we *there* yet?" Once in a while, forgetting that this was a cardinal sin, one of us would sputter it out, only realizing upon hearing the collective hiss of the others' wincing gasps the gravity of the error. My father would let loose a stream of invective, and at that point, all bets were off. If you had to go to the bathroom, you'd better be prepared to drown in it; if you were hungry, get ready to starve. "Are we there yet?" was to my father the most point-less, asinine question anyone could ever ask.

"Is the car still moving? Are we pitching the tent?" These were obvious clues as to the complete and utter absence of *there* in the general vicinity of *where we are* at that particular moment in time. And just to drive home the lesson into the most reptilian recesses of our brains, he promised that if we did reach *there,* he'd roll past it at sixty-five miles per hour, thereby establishing a new *there* that we weren't about to reach anytime soon. So *there.*

My father was King of the Road, and those were his edicts.

We finally reached North Bay, Ontario, nine days after we left BC. As I said, Dad was dubious about the reasons for being dispatched there, but clearly it wasn't because he was desperately needed or because they were waiting for his input. There was no military housing available for us, so we made do with our musky old army tent. For the rest of the summer, and very nearly into the fall, pitched in a campground on the shores of Lake Nipissing, that tent served as our primary residence. My brother slept in the car.

I imagine that my parents were miserable. I'd wake to their tense sotto voce exchanges through the tent walls as they heated coffee on the hibachi. But once again, I viewed it as an extension of the adventure. There were other kids on the site, albeit as vacationers rather than refugees, and a local minor-league team played in a nearby baseball field. I guiltily recall patrolling the stripes of shadow beneath the bleachers with a newfound friend named Spike, collecting nickels and dimes that escaped the pockets of spectators and stealing an occasional illicit glance up the skirts of female fans. My oldest sister, Karen, despondent over leaving behind her boyfriend,

Ed, in British Columbia, was as startled and delighted as my father was disturbed when Ed, a self-described hippie, went on a solo cross-country odyssey of his own and mysteriously arrived at the campsite to whisk Karen away. They were married within the year. In the short term, whatever the family felt about this domestic drama, I think we were all happy to have more room for our sleeping bags. The August heat kindled my parents' urgency to get us kids settled into permanent housing in time for school in September—something more than canvas between their family and the chill of the Northern Ontario autumn or, God forbid, winter.

They found a modest three-bedroom bungalow near the semi-rural, backwater town of Callander, Ontario, birthplace of the Dionne quintuplets. The next year, we moved into PMQs (private military quarters). Two years later, in 1971, Dad jumped at his first opportunity to retire with a pension. Our family loaded back into the Pontiac to do the whole thing once more, only in a westwardly direction. Karen and Ed, married by now with a kid of their own, were already in BC. Steve, a recent high school graduate, well accustomed to a peripatetic lifestyle, was touring Europe with friends, carrying backpacks affixed with Canadian flags to avoid arguments about Vietnam. This time it was Jackie, now fifteen, who was leaving a boyfriend behind, whom I remember as a really cool guy with a supercharged Plymouth Barracuda.

All those years ago, I made up my mind that should I ever have kids of my own, I would one day drag their asses across the continent. It was just a question of when, how, why, where from, and where to.

Are We There Yet?——Redux

CONNECTICUT · JUNE 7, 1997

If I can't build this goddamn boat, I decided, *the car trip is off.*

It was the first weekend in June of 1997; the following Monday would be my thirty-sixth birthday. On the following Tuesday, Sam and I, along with my friend John and his two kids, Emily and Josh, slightly older and slightly younger than Sam, respectively, would climb into a brand-spanking-new Chevy Suburban and set off on a sixteen-day excursion across the United States. But faced with a dizzying array of marine superstructure and entrails—the hull, the propeller, the drive shaft, the power plant, the decking, and the wheelhouse—laid out in front of me, I could feel doubt gathering in my mind as to whether the trip would ever take place.

Not that the boat really had anything to do with the car trip. An early birthday gift from a friend on the West Coast, the sporty little power cruiser had been delivered to me on Friday by Federal Express. It was a two-foot-long, assemble-it-yourself scale model—the kind they race in Central Park. The thought behind the gift, I'm sure, was that this was something I could put together with Sam, and the two of us could have fun passing the remote control back and forth as we zipped the little vessel across our Connecticut pond. Let me tell you something, if you think it's difficult to say *toy boat* three times fast, try building one. And if you're up to that challenge, try doing it with Parkinson's.

I opened the kit at my in-laws' dining room table in Connecticut. I took each of the pieces out, cross-checked it against the inventory provided, and tried to identify it from the illustrated instruction sheet. What followed was an exercise in frustration that dragged on for the better (or worst) part of that Saturday morning. For a time, Sam sat at my right hand and did a far better job than I at making sense of the English instructions loosely translated from Japanese. At age eight, he possessed a keener mind for this sort of thing than I ever would, but after an hour or so, it became clear that we weren't going to float this boat anytime soon, and he could find better things to do outside on an early summer morning.

So I sat, paced, muttered, cursed, and more than once came close to sweeping the entire frustrating mess onto the floor. This wasn't gonna happen. This boat would never be built, not by me anyway, and that realization depressed me almost to the point of tears. I blamed my failure to manipulate the various pieces into their designated positions on my Parkinson's-impaired manual dexterity. And my inability to decode the correct method of construction I attributed to the distraction of tremors and the general fog of Parkinson's. Sure, six years out from diagnosis, these were factors, but not to the extent that they are today (twelve years later), and I seldom find myself as maddened and demoralized as I was on that day, trying to float that boat. I'd put more difficult ordeals behind me and would face greater ones in the future, but I took this personally. This challenge spoke to my overall competency as a father. It was a nasty reminder that my health would have an impact on the day-to-day responsibilities I was expected to handle.

Eventually, my mother in-law rescued me from my dark

reverie with a polite reminder that she would be serving lunch soon on that same table, and would I mind taking a break so that she could set the plates out? Only too happy to comply, I dumped the various pieces back in the box, where, to the best of my knowledge, they still remain.

I wondered if I'd allowed myself to fall into a trap. The boat was just a one-off deal, and sure, my condition made it difficult, but let's face it, I was never any good at that kind of thing to start with. My mind quickly raced ahead to the potentially greater trap I may have set for myself—the impending cross-country trip with Sam.

I tried to anticipate every contingency. Reservations had been set for hotels, motels, and the iconic and hard-to-book National Park lodges in Yellowstone and the Grand Canyon; itineraries were locked in; confirmation numbers were confirmed; I'd even consulted long-range weather forecasts. I'd been spoiled with a partner like Tracy, who excelled in attention to detail, so I'd never been one to fret over minutiae. Tracy was torn, I think, between being reassured, even impressed, and being a little unsettled by the thoroughness of my advance work. This zeal for organizing was either a new trait or one I'd been hiding for years, maybe out of concern that once demonstrated, it would come to be expected.

The truth was, I was as surprised by the extent to which I had masterminded and micromanaged this particular expedition as she was. Under normal circumstances, I'm big on vision, but I prefer to delegate the details. Something larger was at work here. Pre-Parkinson's, I relished spontaneity. For every plan A or B, there was a plan C, lacking any specifics other than that it wasn't A or B. I was happy to roll with the punches, go with the flow. In my new life with PD, there not only needs to be a definitive plan C, but a solid plan D, E, and F. It was with that in mind that I threw myself into the planning of The Great Road Trip of '97.

It had been fun to go through the maps and guidebooks with Sam, plot our course, and try to imagine what we would discover along the way. The cross-Canada ramblings of my childhood had made me a lifelong road warrior, and I hoped to promote the same passion in Sam. We already had a history of extended father-son road trips, traveling to Vermont several times and once motoring through the Shenandoah Valley of Virginia with the vague goal of visiting all of the region's underground caves and caverns. The impetus for that particular trip, which also included a stop in Washington, DC (we still have a photo of Sam, myself, George Stephanopoulos, and Bill Clinton clustered around the President's desk in the oval office), had been Sam's last hoorah as an only child. Six years old at the time, he was understandably nervous about the imminent arrival of his twin siblings. We didn't know if they'd be boys or girls, but either way, brothers or sisters, his life was going to change, and it seemed like the appropriate time for some reassuring father-son bonding. Now, two years later, the twins had arrived in the form of Aquinnah and Schuyler, two cherubic little girls, who upon entering any room immediately sucked up all the attention that had heretofore been Sam's alone. Nothing traumatic, but it didn't take an expert to see that his changing role in the family was also having an impact at school.

It wasn't that he rejected change. In fact, he loved change, especially in the form of natural processes, from the caterpillar-cocoon-butterfly metamorphosis to the impact of elements on shaping the earth. A large part of our relationship was based on our mutual fascination with the world around us, how it changed at its own pace and with its own purpose. But the shifting family dynamic as well as the changing expectations at school were difficult to grasp. Then, of course, there was the inexorable change taking place inside of me. While I made no effort to hide the effects of the disease, neither did I make it a topic of daily discussion. Short of forcing a Q & A session that would have done more to raise alarm than evoke answers, it was hard to read Sam's take on my PD. When he did ask about the symptoms, I was always forthright and attempted to present it as, after all, just another natural process. When he saw my fingers shaking, I showed him how he could distract my brain by grabbing and squeezing my hand, thereby interrupting the signal and inducing calm, however short-lived. It was all fine as long as I maintained my poise and tried to view these experiences from his point of view and not project onto him my own anxiety. There were times, however, like when I was wrestling with that fucking boat, that I may have betrayed my own doubts and concerns. What was his take-away from those moments? Was he really drawn by a desire to go outside and play, or was he repelled by this force of change that he couldn't fully understand or fold into any logical process?

After putting the boat in the box and the box on a shelf, I considered my reasons for the cross-country journey I was about to undertake with my son. It was, I decided, about dealing with change by embracing change. If my father's transfer from Chilliwack to North Bay had required me only to board a plane and six hours later to step from one life into another, I think it would have had a radically different effect on me. The week-plus journey by highway and byway (as well as the month spent living Bedouin-style on the shores of Lake Nipissing) allowed me to mark not only the change in my family's environment, but also the shift from the Pacific rain forests to the craggy peaks of the Rockies. We crossed Saskatchewan prairies so flat you could see a grain silo five miles in the distance, and wound our way around the myriad lakes of Manitoba, seeking refuge in our tent from the billions of mosquitoes they spawned. What my mother and father had done, perhaps unwittingly—certainly unwillingly—was put our family's change in the context of a greater transformation happening on every level, everywhere, every day.

This was what our two-week roll across America would be about for Sam and me—the context for the changes in each of our lives. Of course, he just saw it as I did when I was his age: his first Great Road Trip. I, on the other hand, knew that it would probably be my last. That was before 9/11.

NEW YORK CITY · JUNE 10, 1997

Kids are like Labrador retrievers—show them a car with the motor running and the back door open, and giving no thought to the destination, they'll scramble in and hang their head out the window in anticipation of the wind blowing back their hair and whipping the spit off their dangling tongues.

We were embarking on an ambitious odyssey from our apartment on Fifth Avenue to a rented beach house on the Pacific Coast Highway in Malibu, California. Tracy and the twins would fly out shortly after our departure and rendez-vous with us there. Including stops along the way, we gave ourselves approximately sixteen days to get from coast to coast.

The brand-new Chevy Suburban sat at the curb, the chrome and metallic blue paint gleaming in the sunlight of an East Side summer morning. Fresh from the car wash, it wouldn't see soap and water again until California; Sam and I wanted that baby so coated with soot, soil, sand, and splat-tered bug guts that at trip's end we could take a core sample and read the sedimentary layers like a map of where we'd been. Similar guy logic lay behind the overstuffed duffel bags that filled the SUV's "way-back" area—there would be no laundromat visits in Wheeling, West Virginia; Mitchell, South Dakota; Durango, Colorado; or Yuma, Arizona.

The in-dash storage compartment, which my dad had al-ways referred to as the "map box," was especially capacious in my Chevy truck. It held AAA guidebooks and state-by-state road atlases stacked in east-to-west geographical order, lists of contacts along the way, and service and safety infor-mation.

Just before departure, John and I spread our coast-to-coast map of the USA across the hood of the Suburban. For the ben-efit of Tracy and John's wife, Sharon, I traced with my finger the route we'd be taking from New York to Malibu. There was a hell of a lot of country to cover. Our spouses were impressed by our initiative, but happy they'd be flying over us, not driving with us.

We'd motor from New York to Hershey, Pennsylvania, to Columbus, Ohio, to Chicago, through Wisconsin to Minnesota, from the Devils Tower through the Badlands to Deadwood and Mount Rushmore, across Wyoming with a dip into Montana, then south along the Rockies through Colorado, past the Four Corners to the Grand Canyon, and up into Nevada and across California until we hit the beach. We folded the map. I hugged and kissed Tracy and the babies. And we were off!

Not that I held a lingering resentment over Dad's automobilic autocracy. But on this trip, from the start, I resolved to rule with neither an iron fist nor a lead foot. After all, here I was, wanting in a way to replicate the experience for my own son. Now under different circumstances, with a roomier vehicle, a more relaxed timeline, and a bigger budget, I wouldn't need to rely on Dad's old-school methods. So much was different about this trip from the ones I remember as a child. One difference had to do with the fact that there was another family involved; it couldn't hurt to have another licensed driver in the vehicle, some company for Sam, and someone to keep the late-night chatter going when the road got dark and the eyelids got heavy. Sam, Emily, and Josh got along better than I remember my siblings and me doing, although the extra space would go a long way toward keeping the peace. Usually two of the kids would occupy the SUV's first bench position directly behind the driver's seat, and the other would take the farthest bench back for themselves. It was designated "the dump" because the detritus of the day's travel—candy wrappers, apple cores, empty soda cans, and plastic bottles— would wind up there. Anything lost would eventually be found in the dump. Very rarely would John or I venture back there, unless some mystery aroma became so ripe that an adult-supervised cleanup was in order. You never knew what you'd discover back there. Once, after de-trashing the dump, I reported back to John, "I got some good news and some bad news. The good news is, Josh can write his name. The bad news is that he's written it all over the backseat."

Sam's sole conflict with Emily had to do with music. This was before iPods, and my car stereo fairness policy (Dad would never agree to this) meant that we were all forced to listen to Emily's CD of Hanson's "Mmmbop" so many times it was practically a loop. When it was Sam's turn to choose the music, he'd hand me a Clash or Elvis Costello CD—I'd reared him well. While having John and his kids in the car was added value, the trip was, at its core, a father-son experience.

Sam was a honeymoon baby, born in the early summer of '89, less than a year after Tracy and I were married. *Family Ties* was just concluding its seventh and final season; work was under way on *Back to the Future Part II*; and in the early part of 1990, we would transition, with little or no break, into *Back to the Future Part III*. My father passed away that January and suddenly I was a father to a son, but no longer a son to a father. Working, earning a living, and providing for my family became my all-consuming mission. I assumed it had been for my dad as he and my mom raised their brood. I suspect now, though, that Dad, had he still been available for consultation, would have pointed out that he was trying to make ends meet on a military man's salary. I was taking home more in a month than he made in his lifetime. I could do what he could not—slow down, spend time with my wife and son, take advantage of my good fortune. But I was locked into a cycle of working more to work more. During the first years of Sam's life, I was away more than I was at home, and even when Tracy and Sam and my job were all in the same city, as was the case with *The Hard Way,* filmed in New York, my hours were extreme, and family time at a premium.

Then came the Parkinson's diagnosis, an event that, under different circumstances, might have been reason to stop and assess, gain perspective: health, family, career. I didn't do that. I opted for denial, which in my case meant even more work. And when I wasn't on the job, I was drinking. At a time when I needed to draw my family closer, I shut them out. I feared that PD would keep me from being the father and husband I had promised to be. By the mid-nineties, however, I had turned much of this around. I adopted a responsible approach to treating my Parkinson's and quit drinking. And while the films I did still took me away from home on occasion, as in the case of *The Frighteners* in '95, during which I spent six months in New Zealand, my plans for the future were to dramatically increase my time with Tracy, Sam, and my twin baby girls.

In New Zealand, having once again left Tracy alone with not one but three children, I began to envision a return to television and a schedule more amenable to raising a family. I might not have spent as much time with Sam over his first six or seven years as I would have liked, but we had still built a strong relationship. The cross-country trip was not an effort to repair our bond, but to strengthen it.

My dad packed us all in the car not because he wanted to, but because he needed to. Conversely, Sam and I were going not because we needed to, but because we wanted to. Funny, I know if Dad had been around, he would have loved to have been invited along for the ride. Absent an imperative to rush toward his new masters, he would have been free to enjoy all the sidetracks we took, the various odysseys on and off the interstate. He would have laughed at the ridiculous grandeur of the Corn Palace in Mitchell, South Dakota, and he would have found himself just as simultaneously amused and saddened by the bumper sticker we saw in Indiana that announced, "Satan is a faggot." I don't think he would have begrudged Sam and the other kids the countless bathroom stops they required, all of which I happily agreed to, no matter how far out of the way they were or how recent the last one had been. We didn't patronize any fast-food joints (well, maybe one or two), but this was because we had done exhaustive research, charting the best roadside diners in America. At times, though, I did see some merit in Dad's intractable prohibition of the dreaded "Are we there yet?"

"Am I there yet?" was really the question that launched our Suburban across the continent—"there" being the point of no return beyond which Parkinson's dictated the terms of my life. Had the sweeping changes I had instituted—sobriety, a reordering of priorities—come too late? Was there enough of me left to be the man I had never, until now, known that I wanted to be? To say that my attitude toward the disease itself was far less evolved than it is today would be a gross understatement. I still didn't fully own it and was still wrestling with how wholly it owned me. So this journey was, in large part, a rebellion. My maps and lists and contact sheets were preparation, if not for battle, then for some heavy-duty reconnaissance.

I discovered on this trip that maps and borders are arbitrary and often invisible. Without man-made signs, nothing would inform you that you'd transitioned from one place to another. It's all personal perception. Traveling the country coast to coast, I gained an understanding that the ancient, primal boundaries—the Mississippi River, the Continental Divide, the Rocky Mountains, and the Grand Canyon—mark true change. The risk of crossing is rewarded with the discovery of something entirely new and powerful on the other side. Gradually, I relaxed into the idea that what was happening inside of me was only part of my world. The ticking clock that was beginning to create an unhealthy sense of urgency was in fact a metronome that I could dial down to an appropriate tempo. And as for Sam, my present and future traveling companion, I realized that he loved me, trusted me, depended on me, and maybe worried about me a little, but beyond that, I didn't take up too much space in his head. He was having a blast.

Sam did slip a couple of times and ask if we were there yet. One time in particular, as we sped across the grasslands of Wyoming, he began to push the question out of boredom.

Not especially bothered, I nevertheless decided that now would be a good time to nip this in the bud. Without warning, I pulled the car gently over to the side of the road and looked over my shoulder to the backseat. Should I scream? Make threats? Demands? Perhaps take a passive approach, pull out the map, and politely explain our estimated time of arrival for that day, then open the floor up for suggestions on how best to proceed? No. I opted for a different strategy, one Dad would never have conceived of, let alone attempted. I would go all existential on his ass.

"What did you ask me?" I said to Sam, my face and vocal inflection betraying no attitude one way or another.

"Are we there yet?" Sam replied, a bit tentatively now.

"Excellent question." I unbuckled my seat belt and stepped out of the car, maintaining eye contact with him as I rounded the front of the Suburban to the rear passenger door and opened it. "I don't know, Sam," I said, helping him out of his seat and onto the gravel breakdown lane of the otherwise deserted highway. "Let's check it out. Maybe we *are* there."

Surrounding us were empty grasslands as far as the eye could see, interrupted only by the narrow ribbon of concrete upon which we'd been traveling. This was the precise middle of the middle of nowhere. By now John and the kids had climbed out of the car too, and I put it to the group. "What do you guys think, are we there yet? Go ahead. Look around. Take your time."

For the next five or ten minutes, the kids canvassed that enigmatic little tract of dirt, grass, and sagebrush. Emily culled some flowers; Josh found a couple of cool rocks; and Sam returned with what appeared to be a petrified curl of coyote turd. It was primitive psychology, but I was surprised by how well it worked. I think the person most profoundly affected by it was me. We are where we are. If we keep moving, we'll be someplace else. We'll know when we get there.

Epilogue

Tracy Pollan

Eight years ago I retired from *Spin City* and stepped into the great wide open of my post-acting life. I've managed to fill the time or, better put, the time has filled me. I could never have antici- pated just how thoroughly occupied I would be: the Fox Foun- dation, my patient advocacy and political activism, my explorations into the spiritual source of my inspirations and blessings, and, of course, the moment-by-moment celebration that is my family. To paraphrase an old expression, if ten years ago, as I set out upon this second-act odyssey, I had compiled a list of everything I'd hoped to accomplish to this point, I would discover that I had sold myself short.

Even during these last few days of my work on this book, I can reach out and touch, and be assured by, each of the four pillars I have been describing: work, politics, faith, and family. The past week has been, in fact, a perfect representation of the place to which this journey has delivered me, and a promise of where it might carry me still (or not so still).

Dwight, in his mid-forties, is paralyzed from the waist down. Though a former extreme-sports enthusiast and adrenaline junkie, it wasn't his pursuit of high-risk thrills—base-jumping, big-wave surfing, short-track cart racing—that landed him in a wheelchair. Dwight is a victim of more tragically ordinary circumstance. As he was driving home from a late-night pick-up hockey game with his brother and their cousin, their car was T-boned by a drunk in a piss-yellow Hummer. He lost the use of his legs, and the two men with him lost their lives. Right up to that fateful instant at a darkened intersection, his life had been all about pushing boundaries. Then life pushed back. Now he relies on pills, alcohol, bitterness, a cutting wit, and a hard-wired competitive drive to overcompensate for his losses. Dwight is a ticking time bomb.

Or, he would be—if he were a real guy. He's not. To the extent that Dwight exists at all, he's me. He's a character I've been playing on the FX series *Rescue Me* for the last few weeks. My friend Denis Leary, the show's star and writer/producer, called over the summer to feel out my interest in appearing in a four-episode arc. I have done little acting since I retired from *Spin City*—guest roles on *Scrubs* and *Boston Legal*—and neither gig was easy. As an actor with Parkinson's disease, I find it a challenge to play anyone who doesn't have Parkinson's. Acting comes down to choices, and in that I can't always rely on my body to communicate an intention, I'm operating without a full set of tools. Layers of subtext and Stanislavskian sense memory may motivate a character to drink a beer, let's say, but if I can't lift the bottle mouthward without spilling suds, it's all for naught. Dwight presented an especially daunting assignment. He's a paraplegic, for crying out loud, and I'm a human whirligig. How to keep my legs still for more than a few seconds during a take? And, as I said earlier, put me in a chair with wheels and you had best be prepared to chase after me.

Denis was crazy to ask me to do this and I was even crazier to say yes. This is a textbook case of "casting against type," and not only in light of our diametrically opposed physical dispositions. The contrast between Dwight's worldview and my own couldn't be more stark. But, of course, within the context of our differences live our similarities. I know about loss, I know about life rearranged, purpose re-examined, fate's broadsides. After all, I don't do this for a living anymore; I've moved on. But I wasn't evicted, it was my choice. Therefore, I can go back when and if I choose. There are too many reasons to expect that I can pull this off to let Parkinson's convince me that I can't.

And so I took a spin in Dwight's wheelchair. Today, Halloween, is my last day on the set. With only a few scenes left, it's safe to say that I'll survive the experience and make it home in time to trick-or-treat with Esmé, an experience perhaps less survivable than my trick as Dwight. Whether or not the exercise will ultimately be successful rests, I suppose, in the minds of those who take the time to tune in. I'm glad I took the shot, though. One day, I'm sure I'll do it again.

Besides, it keeps my Screen Actors Guild health benefits current.

SATURDAY, NOVEMBER 1, 2008

We wish to remind you that in the timeless tradition of our people, we will observe the **Yahrzeit** *of Karen Lang . . .*

The previous winter, Tracy and I paid a visit to Rabbi Rubinstein's office to discuss arrangements for Aquinnah and Schuyler's upcoming *b'not mitzvah*. Ascribe it to clerical intuition, but the Rabbi quickly sensed that I was preoccupied with something other than the girls' *D'var Torahs*. I told him that I had just recently lost my sister Karen and what a shocking blow it had been to my family. There was nothing practiced or rote about his expressions of compassion and sympathy. So now, a year later, I shouldn't have been at all surprised to learn, in the form of a letter from Central Synagogue, that my sister Karen's name was to be included in the recitation of *Kaddish* during services on Saturday, November 8.

I keep a photograph of K.C. on the desk in my office. I like the picture. It's a candid shot, snapped at a family wedding four months before she died. With just a trace of weariness, she smiles at me from within the rectangle of the frame. At least once a day, five days a week, I smile back. I find it hard to believe those days and weeks have added up to a year since we gathered around Karen's bed and sang our good-byes.

I've come to the synagogue alone. The kids have done the Saturday scatter; sleepovers, ballet lessons, Tracy busy orchestrating pick-ups and drop-offs. But I wanted to be here. So this morning I put on a suit and got into a cab, and now I'm sitting at the end of an empty pew, looking over the order-of-service handed to me by the usher. Karen's is not one of the names on the list being memorialized. I check the date—it is November 1. I am one week early.

The service begins and as it turns out, the nephew of an associate of mine is being *bar mitzvahed* today, so I decide to stick around and see the kid put through his paces. I observe the proud faces of his family and though I've never met this young man, I'm soon *kvelling*, myself. The time comes for the congregation to recite *Kaddish* and the names are read. In a whisper that only she, I, and *Whomever* else is listening can hear, I add Karen's name to the list.

SUNDAY, NOVEMBER 2, 2008

Team Fox, Team Fox . . . clang, clang, clang!

Esmé and I are out on Fifth Avenue urging on the marathoners as they attack the final three-mile stretch to the finish line at Tavern on the Green. The elite runners have long since passed; we're here for the middle-of-the-pack athletes, the lunch bucket crew, the tad-better-than-average grinders who both inspire and shame we nonparticipants.

Specifically, Ez and I root loudest for the 135 competitors running for Team Fox, wearing our foundation's colors and donating the money earned from sponsors to help fund our research programs. Esmé has a keen eye and every time she spies the word "Fox" emblazoned in orange across a blue singlet, she crows, "Team Fox!" and clangs a bloody cowbell that somebody (and I intend to find out who) supplied her with. I mean, I appreciate her enthusiasm, but it would be a little easier to take were she not sitting on my shoulders, all that screaming and clanging within inches of my eardrums.

A coterie of Team Fox family members, staff, and supporters of the foundation have gathered with us at curbside. We're all clapping, whistling, and hoisting banners big and bold enough to be seen by runners still a distance away so that, if necessary, they'll have time to cross to our side of the avenue and run a gauntlet of high fives, the first "five" being mine. Of course, some of our heroes are too dazed, glazed, and distracted by the insipient liquefaction of their guts and bones to even acknowledge the honor guard. But most do, some so fit and relaxed it seems entirely possible that upon reaching Columbus Circle, they could do a lap and sprint the twenty-six miles back to the Verrazano Bridge. One of these specimens is Ryan Reynolds, movie star, recent bridegroom of Scarlett Johansson, and loving son of a PD-afflicted father. Ryan spots us in time to swoop in for some bump-and-run hugs and backslaps, and in appreciation for our mile-twenty-three "attaboys," he would later say, "I gained about fifteen pounds in goose bumps. It kind of pushed me through those last miles."

Ryan's efforts today will bring in over $100,000, adding to our half-a-million-dollar Team Fox total. That's a lot of goose bumps.

This is not the first time that Esmé and I have stood witness to the New York City Marathon as it coursed down Fifth Avenue. Seven years earlier, almost to the day (her birthday is tomorrow), we watched from a hospital room window at Mt. Sinai, just a few blocks north. One day old, enfolded in my arms, not straddling my shoulders, she didn't have a cowbell or the strength to clang one if she did. But now, as she scrambles down from her not-so-lofty perch and smiles up at me as though she's been licked by a puppy, I remember her eyes being just as wide.

MONDAY, NOVEMBER 3, 2008

Esmé has picked her favorite West Side Italian restaurant for her birthday dinner tonight. Tracy made the whole cab ride across the park cradling a white cake box—I certainly couldn't be trusted with it. We have to bring our own homemade birthday cake for Esmé because she has peanut allergies and one can never be sure that peanuts, peanut oil, peanut flour, or some such toxin hasn't found its way into a baker's recipe. Tracy is so cautious about possible contamination from peanuts, she probably wouldn't let them decorate it with an icing Snoopy. We're especially on guard these days, having just done the whole Halloween thing. We had to sort out all the Snickers, Mr. Goodbars, and other nut-based confections from her stash. I'm in charge of that. The offending candies go straight into my desk. Hey, I'm going to need some munchies to calm my nerves while I watch the polls tomorrow night.

TUESDAY, NOVEMBER 4, 2008

Election day, and as has become my custom, I'm out the door early. Owing to the historic nature of this year's presidential contest, and in spite of the fact that here in New York an Obama victory is a lock, my polling station is busier than I've ever seen it. On the steps of the church, a young girl approaches; ten or eleven years of age, she wears a plaid skirt and navy sweater—the uniform of a neighborhood private school. "Excuse me, sir. Can I ask you some questions after you vote?" Looking around, I see that she is one of a contingent of what are easily the world's most irresistible exit pollsters, carrying clipboards and being shadowed by adult overseers. "Sure," I respond. Obviously they're conducting research as part of a civics class, but it occurs to me that this would be a brilliant firewall against the "Bradley effect." Who could lie to these kids?

Inside there are plenty of smiles. Everybody is happy. I sign in, enter the booth, draw closed the curtain, flick my favorite switches, and pull the lever. I'm reasonably happy myself.

Back outside, my student statistician and her teacher wave me over and run through a series of questions, each of my answers dutifully transcribed. "You don't have to answer this last one if you don't want to," she says tentatively, like I wouldn't be willing to give the kid my social security number at this point. "May I ask how you voted for president?" "I'll give you a hint," I respond, opening my leather jacket to reveal a T-shirt given to me by my friend Nelle. The subtly modified version of a stylized orange movie logo is instantly familiar to the little girl's teacher. Upon reading it, she quickly glances up again at my face as her pupil sounds out the words: "Barack to the Future." Now the teacher is laughing. It's become clear to both of us that her young charge doesn't get the reference, and I have a pretty good laugh too.

I saw, during the midterm campaign of 2006, how difficult it was for opponents of stem cell research to run against hope. And so it was in the 2008 presidential contest. This was hope in the collective, a definition that should always apply to the expression of a people's political will. Christopher Reeve had believed in a formula: optimism + information = hope. In this case, the informing agent was *us*. Granted, it may all look different in six months to a year, but it is hard not to be buoyed by the desire for positive change as articulated and advanced by Barack Obama. It is okay to hope. This time the aspiration of many will not be derided as desperation by a few, as it was during the stem cell debate of '06.

By the time you read this book, President Obama and the 111th Congress will have established federal funding for stem cell research. The dam has broken.

Just as I'd hoped.

WEDNESDAY, NOVEMBER 5, 2008

"This is almost worth getting Parkinson's for!" I announce to the thousand or so who have gathered in the ballroom of the Sheraton Midtown for the Michael J. Fox Foundation's annual fund-raising benefit, *A Funny Thing Happened on the Way to Cure Parkinson's*. Already fired up, the crowd understands exactly what I'm talking about, and they send up a roar. I step back from the microphone and adjust the tone and volume knobs on the 1962 sunburst Les Paul guitar that Tracy gave me a few Christmases back. I don't think of myself as one who prizes possessions, but if I do have a prized possession, this fine piece of American musical craftsmanship is definitely it. The guitar deserves better than me, but I love to play it, even when I'm locked up and quaking, unable to regulate a strumming rhythm with my right arm or describe a chord pattern or lead line to the fret-board with the failing fingers of my left hand. Sometimes I just cradle the Gibson, and in the tradition (if not exactly the spirit) of generations of rock and roll guitarists the world over, I wait for the drugs to kick in.

Tonight though, I'm ready, my symptoms are well under control, and if I do happen to falter, I can count on the boys in the band to carry me for a bar or two. The song is "Magic Bus." The band is The Who. That's right, I've just joined Pete Townshend and Roger Daltrey onstage for their encore after a rousing performance to benefit PD research. I look to Pete as he rolls out the growling, Bo Diddley shuffle in A that drives the bus. I'm stunned and amazed to find myself joining in, just as, from somewhere behind me, stage left, Roger rasps, "Every day I get in the queue . . ." See what I'm saying? *This is almost worth getting Parkinson's for.*

I could make the same statement about the events that led me to the formation of an organization that has done so much to advance research into the relentless and debilitating condition affecting millions of people around the world. The effort and achievement is not mine, but must be credited to Debi Brooks and her successor, the dynamic and driven Katie Hood, our staff, our board of directors, scientists, and the thousands who recognize the importance of our work and encourage us through financial and emotional support. By the spring of 2009, the foundation will have funded nearly two hundred million dollars in Parkinson's research, making it the leading private organization of its kind.

Even in this period of extreme economic turmoil, with much of our support from the beleaguered financial industry, we expect tonight to raise as much as in previous versions of this event, in excess of four million dollars. In fact, the total will climb unexpectedly in a few days, when the *New York Times'* special "Giving" section features a cover article detailing the foundation, its work, and its groundbreaking approach to pushing science forward:

What makes the story of the Michael J. Fox Foundation different—nay, what makes it important—is that it doesn't just dole out money to scientists and hope for the best. It has used its money to take control of Parkinson's research like few other foundations have ever done. In the process of trying to solve the mysteries of Parkinson's, it has upended the way scientific research is done, and the way academics interact with pharmaceutical and biotech companies, at least in its little corner of the world. It demands accountability and information sharing that is almost unheard of in the broad scientific community. And it has managed to become, in its short life, the most credible voice on Parkinson's research in the world.

Back on stage, Roger is dripping sweat and, microphone and harmonica wedged between praying hands, honking and blowing through the harmonica break in "Magic Bus." As Zach Starkey (Ringo Starr's kid) kicks the rumble of the drums up another decibel or two, Pete Townshend and I build to the crescendo with a series of power chords. I'm standing and playing my beloved Les Paul, not three feet away from one of the greatest rock legends of all time. As he begins to wind into the first of a series of his patented windmills, he smiles and nods for me to do likewise. It's been a long time since Marty McFly paid homage to Townshend with the same move in *Back to the Future*, but it worked then, so I screw up the courage to try it again now. My arm wheels around like a board-game spin-arrow. This is nuts. I take in the throng of people who have pressed to the edge of the stage, and immediately recognize the beautiful faces of Aquinnah and Schuyler. The girls are rockin' out. Even though it's a school night, they have been allowed to attend the benefit for the first time this year. Esmé is of course at home, asleep, dreaming up tomorrow's cockamamie scheme. Sam, alas, away at college, has missed the spectacle, but he'll be sick of hearing me talk about it soon enough.

Now I catch sight of Tracy. I think I'll have a roadie go out and slip her a backstage pass. She looks especially fine.

THURSDAY, NOVEMBER 6, 2:00 ..

Too much. Magic bus!

My rock star fantasy is a few hours behind me, and I am back at home with my family. It's still a school night, so Aquinnah and Schuyler quickly go into their room to slip out of their party dresses, emerging in the pajamas that have them looking like the little girls they will always (sorry, it's a Dad thing) be to me. Hugs and good-night kisses and then, within minutes, the sounds from behind their door go from giggles to snores.

Half an hour later, Tracy (my one and only groupie) and I say our good-nights and then, once she is asleep, I get out of bed and commence my night wandering. It is my regular pattern. Sleep, like waking, is not something I can sneak up on. It's a negotiation, seeking consensus among all the bickering factions—mind, body, psyche—before I can simply lie down, close my eyes, and drift off to sleep.

Accomplishing all that I needed and wanted to in the preceding hours required a greater than usual amount of medication, and I'm paying for it now with dyskinesias. I shuffle throughout the apartment, to the fridge for water, back to my den to check my e-mail. Someone's already forwarded a picture of me with Roger, Pete, and the boys, lifted from a wire service. I'm physically exhausted by now, my face too mask-like to approximate the ecstatic smile the photo-me beams out from the Mac. I feel it emotionally, though; my adrenaline from the night's events will add an hour or so to my nocturnal ritual. The trick is to hit the sack at the ideal moment, when my last, slightly reduced round of meds has kicked in and I can climb under the covers without stirring Tracy with too much kicking and shaking.

I enter our bedroom and feel my way around the edges of the bed. My balance, compromised at the best of times by Parkinson's, is in this darkness wholly unreliable. If I do stumble, at least I'll pitch forward onto the bed, insuring a soft landing. Rounding the turn to my side, I glide my barely tremulous hand under the hem of the coverlet, ready to flip it back and climb in. When my feet touch the shoes, pre-set for the morning, I know I'm in the right position. We're feather mattress and down comforter people, so I curl in under the covers like a cat on a cushion. I silently thank Tracy for the warmth; the last thank-you to my wife of the day, and the latest of millions over the course of our life together.

After all the work it took me to get here, I'll fall asleep in no time. It's likely that I'll get up a few times, perhaps in as soon as an hour. I'll reprise my wandering-almost-Jew routine, but only for a few minutes. And then I'll return to bed and nod off again. In between, as I sleep, there will be the "mind movies." When prescribing one of the drugs I take, my doctor warned me of a common side effect: exaggerated, intensely vivid dreams. To be honest, I've never really noticed the difference.

I've always dreamt big.

Acknowledgments

With love and gratitude I'd like to acknowledge the following for their personal support and for their contributions to this book.

Tracy—you make it all go. Twenty-plus years, and with every day I fall in love with you all over again.

Sam, Aquinnah, Schuyler, Esmé, thank you for your understanding and inspiration. I love each and every one of your guts.

Thank you to my mom, Phyllis, for having me and for everything you've done since.

In this endeavor, as in all things, I've benefited from the close relationships I've maintained with my smart, funny, and spirited siblings: my brother, Steve; my sisters Kelli, Jackie, and K.C. (whom we all miss terribly).

Thank you as well to the world's greatest in-laws, Corky and Stephen Pollan.

I couldn't have survived this experience day in and day out without the enthusiasm, intelligence, and support of my writing assistant, Asher Spiller.

Mired in one of my many bouts of writer's block, I complained to Tracy, "I'm never going to finish my book on optimism." "What you need," she advised me, "is someone to crack the whip every day." And so I reached out to the person Tracy suggested, my trusted producing partner, Nelle Fortenberry. Nelle, without you this task would have been hopeless.

I was also lucky enough to have access to the brilliance of two solid pros, my brother-in-law, the legendary Michael Pollan, and the accomplished political journalist Frank Wilkinson.

My deepest appreciation goes out as well to Jackie Hamada, Nina Tringali, Iwa Goldstein, and Patti Ruiter, all of whom kept my life and office running while I was busy trying to recapture memories from the campaign trail and other events of the last ten years.

Hyperion has been such an outstanding partner, and I'm grateful for everyone's patience and unflagging belief in *Always Looking Up*. Leslie Wells, as she was with *Lucky Man*, has been the ideal editor and mentor. I want to thank Bob Miller for bringing me back to Hyperion for another go-around, and Ellen Archer for jumping in with energy and insight. Thanks also to Marie Coolman and Leslie Sloane for supporting the book's launch.

I want to thank the staff, board, scientific advisors, and supporters of the Michael J. Fox Foundation for Parkinson's Research for their generosity, commitment, and belief in our mission. Of particular assistance to me during the writing of this book were Debi Brooks, Katie Hood, Todd Sherer, Brian Fiske, Kate Gendreau, Holly Barkhymer, Sandy Drayton, and Karen Leies. I am grateful to them for their comments and contributions.

ACKNOWLEDGMENTS

Many people made themselves available to me during my writing process, sharing their insight, personal experience, and stories of inspiration: Bishop Carlton Pearson, George Stephanopoulos, Lance Armstrong, Lonnie and Muhammad Ali, Rabbi Rubinstein, Donny Deutsch, Lawrence O'Donnell, Mike Manganiello, Claire McCaskill, Sherrod Brown and Connie Schultz, Ben Cardin, Jim Doyle, and Tammy Duckworth.

My agent, the one and only Binky Urban, thank you. John Rogers, my guide through all things political, thank you. Thanks as well to your assistant Kelly and crack staff. My appreciation to Dr. Susan Bressman and Mark Seliger for their contributions. To Bob Philpott, Aaron Philpott, Peter Benedek, and Cliff Gilbert-Lurie, thanks for taking care of business.

Special mention to Bruce Springsteen, Pete Townshend, and Roger Daltrey. Curtis and Carolyn Schenker, you guys are the best friends anyone could ask for. Denis Leary, thanks for making me laugh. And for the job. Mort Kondracke, see you at lunch in November of 2010. And of course, much love and gratitude, as always, to Joyce A.

I could devote as much time to this list as I did to the book itself, and still it would never be truly complete. There are so many who have been a part of this journey, and if you do not see your name here, know that it is written on my heart.